THE WILL TO CREATE

THE WILL TO CREATE

LLADRÓ®

© Lladró Comercial, S.A.
Ctra. de Alboraya, s/n
Tavernes Blanques, Valencia (Spain)
ISBN: 84.605.7557.8
Depósito legal: V-1959-1998
Printed by: Artes Gráficas Fernando Gil
Printed in Spain

CONTENTS

I. THREE LIVES, ONE PATH

II. A DAY IN THE LIFE OF THE CITY OF PORCELAIN

III. UNIVERSAL ARTWORK

IV. SOURCES OF INSPIRATION

V. LLADRÓ IN WORLD MUSEUMS

The testimonies offered in this book are just a sample of the many experiences that could be recounted by both the Lladró brothers and their most veteran associates. The staunch support of these associates and the recollections of the protagonists of this real-life story – Juan, José and Vicente Lladró – have been combined to make this work possible.

THE WILL TO CREATE

"We want our creations to be elegant, expressive, brimming with life; we want them to have feeling. We want them to reflect the good side of life, showing positive human values and everything that ennobles our existence. There is enough pain in the world already. We reject all forms of discrimination, we detest violence and evil and we try to bring out the best in human beings." These words from Vicente, the youngest of the founding brothers of the Lladró company, sum up the exact meaning of their life and work. His statement is particularly suited to the commencement of this work because it underlines the fact that Lladró is above all a famous name that stands for fine art, and although it is now the trademark it was originally a surname of a family whose story is told here, without which it would be impossible to recount the history of the most famous porcelain figurines in the second half of the twentieth century. This is the story of the men who gave porcelain a new name, the story of

Juan, José and Vicente Lladró.

Juan Lladró

José Lladró

Vicente Lladró

When the Lladró brothers first began to make their way in a difficult world, an artistic vocation drove them to embark on an arduous yet fascinating journey. The three Lladró brothers

1. THREE LIVES, ONE PATH

displayed a determination to succeed which has never abandoned them.

By deciding to combine their talents they were unwittingly laying the foundations of an ambitious project: a major venture whose creations were destined to be admired by porcelain art lovers the world over.

This story, in which enterprising self-made men succeed in building an empire with their own hands, has three special protagonists: Juan, José and Vicente Lladró. The cast has now incorporated a second generation of men and women who have not forgotten their origins, and like their elders, have made porcelain art a way of life.

Valencia, Spain. The 1940's. Spaniards were struggling to improve their lot in the aftermath of the Spanish Civil War which had devastated the fibre and the economy of a nation. With circumstances against them, three brothers born into a humble farming family fought in their own way to improve their lives.

Three Lives, One Path

THE BEGINNINGS OF A VOCATION

"The world in which we grew up and were educated was very difficult," says Juan, the eldest of the three brothers. "We suffered many hardships. You have to remember that we lived through most of the war and were severely affected by it in the years that followed. All the possessions our family had were a few acres of land which was not enough for us to subsist on. Our father had to go out to work in a foundry, and we had to help him on the farm. This is how we made ends meet. At school, as I recall, we didn't even have paper to write on; there weren't enough teachers because most of the men had been drafted during the war, including schoolteachers, so we were lucky to have obtained at least some semblance of a primary education. I remember one day how the schoolteacher gave me a box of used paints which I kept throughout my childhood. Maybe he did this to awaken my interest in drawing, or perhaps he simply didn't have anything else to give me, I don't know."

This story could be considered as a premonition. The brothers' true artistic vocation, as they remember it, grew from necessity rather than anything else. The circumstances of their life brought about an urge for improvement that awakened their creative spirit.

"The idea of taking up studies," in the words of Juan, "came to us as we got older. It was our mother who encouraged us to get

The Lladró brothers were born in this house in Almácera, a small town in the Valencian 'huerta'.

a better education, as she knew we would have to get out into the world and make a better start. At first I wanted to be a draughtsman, but when my mother found a job for me as a decorator, I switched from draughtsmanship to artistic drawing because I wanted to specialize in something. It wasn't really part of the plan for me to become an artist."

Left, José and Juan posing for their first communion. Above, Vicente as a child.

The boys' father, Juan Lladró. "We had to help our father on the farm, and he had to go out to work in a foundry as well. This is how we made ends meet."

The boys' mother, Rosa Dolz. "It was our mother who encouraged us to never argue amongst ourselves and to always work together. Thanks to her advice, we were able to succeed."

In 1942 Juan started work as a painter of ceramic tiles and dishes in a local factory, and a year and a half later, his brother José followed suit. José reminisces on this period as follows:

IN SEARCH OF A PROFESSION

"We worked in a department where plates were made, which we then decorated with simple motifs. It was here, at sixteen years of age that I earned my first paypacket. It was a very small wage – we were paid less than the more experienced workers. It was a very repetitive kind of job. But we formed part of a group of young people with artistic yearnings, which we nurtured by attending the local Arts and Crafts School. On Sundays, my brother Juan and I would spend the day painting still lifes, landscapes, and people from the 'huerta' – either in oils or watercolours."

Their good grades at school reflected their artistic vocation. Encouraged by their successes and the awards they were given, the two elder brothers started studying painting and decorative composition in addition to artistic drawing. Vicente, who was younger, entered school later on.

The Valencia School of Arts and Crafts, where the three brothers received their thorough artistic training.

"Don Salvador Tuset, our teacher, valued my skills as a painter very highly," affirmed Vicente. "He liked the way I used blurring effects in my compositions, and advised me to study painting, but I told him that I wanted to complement the work my brothers were doing by taking up sculpture, since they preferred being painters."

Little by little the pathways being prepared by the three brothers began to fuse into one, thanks to the foresight of their mother and her wish to see them succeed. A closely-knit family was being consolidated and would soon prove to be indestructible. Vicente remembers this himself, referring to times of crisis:

A self-portrait painted in oil by Juan Lladró when he was young.

"Our mother would always insist that we try not to argue amongst ourselves and continue to work side by side. Thanks to this, we managed to stick together."

The two elder brothers began to study ceramics as well. Their tile factory jobs were simply not enough for their aspirations, and little by little they began to look farther afield. This is the way Juan described it:

"In the tile factory, we did routine work. There was very little variety among models, we did mostly the same thing all the time. Because of this, we began to take advantage of our free time to start testing things out for ourselves. For example, we ate our sandwiches in only ten minutes and used the remaining twenty minutes of our lunch break to experiment and test out our ceramic techniques. At night, the kiln managers at the factory itself fired our first pieces for us, so that we could check the results. We have portraits, landscapes and copies of pictures on tiles or plates from that time which are now preserved in our museum."

A group of "arts and crafts" students and artists on a field trip. Juan and José Lladró are standing, the second and fourth respectively from left to right.

"We also experimented at home," remembers José. "Since we were not able to do all our firing work in the tile factory, we asked a bricklayer to build a small, Moorish-style kiln for us, but it did not work very well and we then constructed another wood burning kiln. To buy our fuel we had to sell the oxen we kept at home."

Their growing activities in ceramics gave them problems at work. Their will to succeed pushed them relentlessly towards total independence.

"We started having problems at the company where we were working," said Juan. "There was no room

Self-portrait in oil painted by José, from the same period as his brother Juan's.

for improvement, there were no jobs that enabled us to sharpen our skills. We wanted to do better, to become true professionals. This is why we built a kiln at home, to experiment and get more involved in the trade. At the company they thought we wanted to compete with them, but the only thing we really wanted was to learn, to broaden our experience. This is why we finally had to leave the tile factory."

Above, a shot of the classroom at the Arts and Crafts School where the Lladró brothers were studying. Right, three examples of studies done by the Lladró brothers, while receiving their formal artistic training there.

Self-portrait sculpted by Vicente, who decided to specialize in sculpture to complement his brothers' artistic abilities.

THE FIRST WORKS. *While they were working in a tile factory, the Lladró brothers dedicated their free time to making pieces like these, dating from the 1940s. These pieces, decorated and fired by the Lladró brothers themselves, are examples of how they developed their artistic capacities and made progress in the field of ceramics. Some of the themes appearing in these works would follow the Lladró brothers throughout their career, such as the Don Quixote motif shown below.*

Above left, "Advice to Sancho", ceramics decorated on-glaze by Juan Lladró. Right, "Village", a plate made using the same technique by José Lladró. Below left, "Old Man", painted by José. Above, "The Portrait" with under-glaze decoration by Juan.

PARENTAL SUPPORT. The history of the Lladró brothers is the history of a family. In their early years, Juan, José and Vicente received support, advice and guidance from their parents, who helped them through many difficult times. The three works on this page pay tribute to the love and gratitude the three brothers have always shown towards their parents – Valencian farmers whose strong family ties gave rise to the subsequent success of the Lladró company throughout the world.

Busts of their parents, sculpted by Vicente, and a small portrait of their mother, painted on ceramics by Juan, are two examples of the early artistic talents shown by the Lladró brothers.

They embarked on a time of uncertainty, a time in which they had to struggle to survive. Vicente, who in view of his youth, had only worked on the farm up until this time, now joined his brothers and shared in some of the tasks of making ceramics. They tried to sell what they produced, and in fact, they still remember with great appreciation how some friends of theirs bought a ceramic piece every now and then to help them. The homemade kiln was not always successful in firing, and the neighbours occasionally complained about the smoke those Lladró brothers were always making. Vicente remembers that trying time during which they moved slowly forward:

"There was a time when we thought we would have to quit, with each of us setting out on our own, in view of all the problems we had: people complaining

Three Lives, One Path

THE START OF AN ADVENTURE

A view of the Valencian huerta, the scene of the Lladró brothers' youth.

about the smoke, our lack of experience, our repeated failures... It was our mother who calmed things down and encouraged us to continue, insisting that we remain united. And eventually we made it."

"Suppliers did not trust us. We were unknown, so in order to get hold of raw materials, we had to go personally to a supplier, pay cash and take our materials away by our own means, usually on our backs. I used to travel to Manises to get glaze materials, load myself up with 30 to 40 kilograms, and use public transport to get home. We brought other products from the city, using a cart we pulled ourselves. We would see our friends go by, carrying their books to school, whereas I would be coming from the opposite direction pulling a cartload of alabaster, thinking about how to get it onto a local train with-

Above, a Moorish kiln like this one was where the first Lladró creations were fired. Below, in a photo from the forties, the Manises tram. As Vicente recollects: "We would see our friends go by, carrying their books to school, whereas I would be coming from the opposite direction pulling a cartload of alabaster, thinking about how to get it onto a local train."

© PHOTO: CARLOS SANCHIS - MANISES.

23

out having to pay the freight costs, thereby saving a few pesetas."

"In our early days we made lots of things, like little flowers, ashtrays, vases and candleholders... One of us modelled, another painted, and the third fired the pieces... They were objects that we sold at any price we could, to get some more money to buy materials. These are the objects we are currently trying to recover, and quite often, their current owners do not want to sell them, arguing that if it is our pleasure to exhibit them in a museum, it happens to be their pleasure to have them adorning their privates houses." In addition to working for the public, the Lladró brothers worked for themselves, fueling their passion for porcelain. As José remembers, they started accumulating lots of objects, obliging their mother to distribute them throughout the house, which was filled up with their initial creations, reflecting all their enthusiasm and joi-de-vivre, irrespective of their skills, techniques and knowledge.

Some of the Lladró brothers' very own first creations are still on exhibit in the Lladró Center in New York.

The sculpture crowning this piece from 1950 is the work of Vicente Lladró, whereas the flowers and the decoration are by José.

Around this time, chance so had it that a porcelain insulator factory located in their home town decided to open up an artistic porcelain department. Since the owners knew about the activities of the three brothers, they hired José first, and then Juan, who was doing his military service at the time, and later Vicente. In all they worked there for four years, during which time they began to acquire greater knowledge of their trade.

Three Lives, One Path

THE TURNING POINT

Above, a vase decorated with flowers by Juan and a rococo scene painted by José. Below, young Juan Lladró working in the ceramics factory where he decorated pieces.

"In Spain the porcelain factories of old had disappeared," recalled Juan, "so this was going to be the only one. We played a decisive role in the development of the company as a manufacturer of porcelain figurines. The artistic director, Don Vicente Beltrán, supervised our work and taught us to do our very best. He was an intelligent man, very demanding with himself and with others. We possessed a knowledge of decorative techniques that he lacked, but by working side by side we got better and better in all respects. We asked the owners for better pay in exchange for full-time work but they didn't want to give us any more money. Finally we decided we had to go. They thought they could replace us with other people, but the facts show that this was never the case. They began to decline after we left."

This time, however, they adapted to the situation much more easily than in the past. Now they possessed the keys to their trade. The only thing they needed was to make a decision. And this is what they did.

"We had two options," said Juan, "either we had to start looking for other jobs or we had to start our own team and dedicate all our efforts to porcelain making. So we decided to do the latter."

They got together a small group of acquaintances: Manolo Leonor, whom they had met at the School of Arts and Crafts, Fulgencio García, a sculptor who had left the factory two years before them, and a number of other people from the neighbourhood were taken on as workers. Over the

years many of these people achieved a high degree of specialization, and in some cases, they reached positions of responsibility within the company.

Each of the three brothers had his own job to do. Juan took charge of decorating figurines, managing the laboratory and administration. Vicente was responsible for glazing, moulds and firing. José coordinated manufacturing and staff relations. All three of them were involved in the creative process, however. Their workday was long, from dawn to dusk, the rhythm was set by demand, and demand was always high. The tiny workshop they founded began to produce figurines depicting a variety of themes: flowers, ballerinas, compositions with animals, traditional Valencian

Above, a shot of the first Lladró stand at the Valencia Trade Fair. Below left, José Lladró in the workshop founded by the three brothers after they left their jobs as employees at a ceramics factory. Right, Vicente Lladró in a photo from the same period.

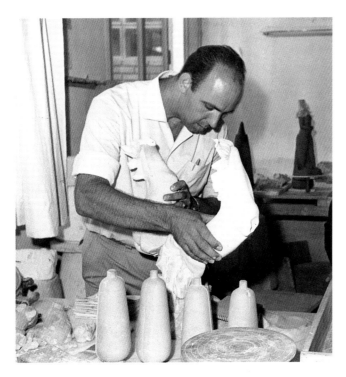

figurines, angels, vases, and so on. They sold these systematically, attending trade fairs and travelling to other cities in Spain carrying their pieces with them.

"At first, we didn't go to trade fairs to offer our products," recounted José, "but just to look, to see what others did. The first time we went out to sell we had five or six samples with us in a suitcase, because we had no catalogues or even photographs. People liked our work because our pieces were very well made, and this was even before the pieces had their own style. Perhaps the success of these initial pieces was due to the fact that artworks of this kind were not generally available to people in Spain, but I think it was also because there was something special about them."

With the proceeds they obtained from the sale of porcelain flowers, the Lladró brothers made ends meet and managed to make investments in their

Juan, Vicente and José, with some of their first associates, at the door of their parents' home where they first set up shop. Standing on the far right is Juan Lladró, the brothers' father.

workshop. At this time there were very few models, not enough to make a catalogue, and the first commercial agents to work for the Lladró brothers had to carry original pieces around to show to potential customers. This gave potential buyers a chance to see the natural grace of these figurines for themselves. It was not easy to sell a luxury product at that time. They had to be affordable, so artistic aspects had to be combined with efficient techniques to highlight the beauty of the early Lladró models.

Above, one of the first catalogues used by the Lladró brothers to illustrate their creations. Left, a piece from 1956 decorated by Juan Lladró. Due to limited production at the first Lladró studio, these pieces have become prized collector items over the decades.

Three Lives, One Path

IMPROVING DAY BY DAY

Initially, both economic and technical limitations obliged the Lladró brothers to work with ceramic materials. This material is fired at a temperature of around 1,000°C (1,832°F) and consists of clay and water to which other elements are added to achieve specific colours. A material of this kind falls short of reaching the type of quality and nuances provided by hard porcelain, and this is why the brothers felt there was a shortfall between the artistic quality of their models and the materials they employed at that time. They began to realize that they needed a better base material for their creations, and so replaced their old wood-burning kiln with a newer kiln which was capable of achieving temperatures above 1,300°C (2,372°F) as required for the production of true porcelain.

Although they had already worked with porcelain before, they had used it for artistic purposes only and still did not have a full command of all the technical aspects of production. Yet soon after they began hiring salesmen to help them to sell their creations, demand started increasing, and as Juan remembers it, problems got bigger and bigger:

"The wood-burning kiln was second hand and was not very well built, but we thought we could fix it. We made some escape channels which turned out to be too long and we ended up cracking the inside of the kiln. After a number of modifications we finally got it to work. Another difficulty was the porcelain we bought, which was very hard to work with. So what we did was go to a friend of ours who was a

The first major advance in the Lladró brothers' career was the change from ceramics to porcelain. Shown left is "Valencian Girl", a figurine made in glossy ceramics and decorated on-glaze by Juan Lladró. To the right is a view of the old steel mills of Sagunto. The Lladró brothers constructed their first kiln using refractory materials from this foundry.

pharmacist and ask him to research what we could add to the mixture to make it more workable without losing any of its other qualities. After testing out various products, we used an additive which worked for us for well over five years. In the end we even had our supplier wondering what was going on. Today, the name of the material is not important, but in those days our secret recipes enabled us to keep the boat from sinking."

"We made improvements day after day," added Vicente. "After the wood-burning kiln we decided to build a better kiln. We picked up old refractory materials from the steel mills of Sagunto – they were really fragments of refractory bricks which we tried to clean as best we could so that we could fit them together. They did not often stick together long, and our kiln lost lots of heat. Firing in the kiln is extremely impor-tant because it is the last step in the process, and if you don't get it exactly right, all your work is point-less. To fire porcelain the kiln has to reach the maximum temperature the material can with-stand. If you don't reach the right temperature the texture will not be fine enough, and if you overshoot the right temperature your fig-urine will crack. I started specializing in making kilns and my brothers spe-cialized in chemistry. All three of us continued to work on design."

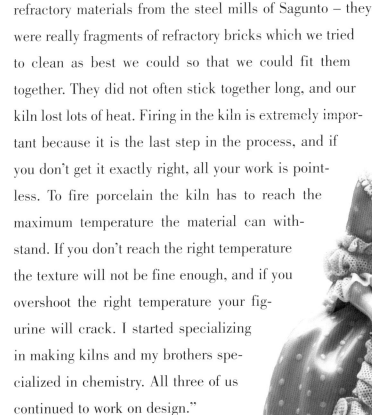

"The Ball", a porcelain figurine made soon after the ceramic figurine shown on the preceding page.

TEAMWORK. When qualified chemists joined the team, great advances were made in perfecting porcelain paste and the use of pigments. The Lladró laboratory became a centre for experimentation, and new developments and techniques were discovered that enabled artists to give material form to the fruits of their imagination. Above left, Adolfo Pucilowsky and Claudio Guillém. Right, Ramón Gil.

The Lladró brothers brought together a group of artists and sculptors who shared the same tastes, inspiration and dedication. These were the key factors which made it possible for such a complete range of work to be produced over the years without losing any of the common traits that make these creations unmistakably Lladró.

Fulgencio García.

Julio Ruiz.

Salvador Furió.

Juan Huerta.

Vicente Martínez.

Francisco Catalá.

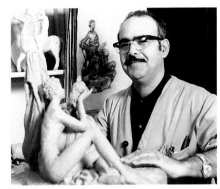

Julio Fernández.

Antonio Ballester.

Salvador Debón.

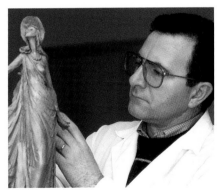

José Puche.

The Lladró brothers were able to gather together an outstanding group of artists, painters and sculptors – talented artists in their own right – who contributed their devotion and skills to a common project led by the three brothers. Perhaps the Lladró brothers' most significant virtue was their ability to transmit their exceptional enthusiasm and their personal view of art to this team. In this way their art became rich and varied while still preserving coherence and unity. This page shows the pioneers, the members of the first team of artists trained by the Lladró brothers, many of whom are still active. Later, other artists joined the team, and today they still continue cultivating the style and know-how that grew up around the first team of specialists.

There was a growing need to hire people with technical know-how, bringing their skills to bear within the expanding group of Lladró associates. In the late fifties, the Lladró brothers met Adolfo Pucilowsky, a chemist of Polish origin, who had been working in some of the small ceramics companies in Manises. The artistic team, meanwhile, was reinforced by the arrival of Julio Fernández first of all, and then Julio Ruiz.

WORKING TO INNOVATE

"We then decided to decorate under the glaze," stated José. "We had already done this in ceramics, but not in porcelain. Using Pucilowsky's suggestions, we created a new system that greatly improved our work methods."

"We experimented a lot with colours. I remember how after seeing a finished piece representing a deer being pursued by a group of three dogs painted in colourful tones, I decided to paint the scene following a personal inspiration. I used grey, beige and browns for the deer and the dogs. I had only recently discovered the attractiveness of grey tones. It was a rainy day and I had gone out into the country to paint. The landscape had an ashy hue and my canvas reflected a whole range of cool tones, leaden tones, with all the colours softened by the grey sky. Those memories of such an unusally sunless day in Valencia were what I tried to bring into this new piece I was creating, and we all agreed that it worked, it seemed to idealize the sculpture, make it more natural, more spiritual."

"After seeing a colourful piece representing a deer being chased by some hounds, I decided to paint another version following a personal inspiration," recollects José Lladró.

This chromatic transformation experienced by Lladró creations was accompanied by another no less dramatic change that affected the moulding process. Juan tells us about it.

"The pieces we created at first were firmly set within the European porcelain making tradition of old, but then we started doing something different, making them more modern looking, more innovative, within the prevalent fifties style of straight lines. We made two or three models that no one seemed to appreciate, and then we finally got it right with a harlequin much like a Picasso creation, which we made using elongated shapes. I remember that García, one of our artists, liked well-rounded forms, and it was difficult for him to understand what we wanted, but eventually he came up with stylized pieces which looked a little out of proportion but showed lots of sensitivity. At first our customers raised their eyebrows, because they weren't sure these pieces were going to please the public, but they soon saw that they did. It was in this way that we created a style of our own, a style that characterized us for quite some time."

What motivated the Lladró employees the most was the fact that they worked in an organization that helped them in their personal development, using guidelines from above without strict impositions. As a result of this climate propitiating creativity, everyone became involved in the creation and perfection of stylized figurines with a kind of decoration that was appropriate for the new style. European porcelain was using practically the

same colour palette as always, even though it was technically possible to create a much wider range of tones. This was the case at the Lladró laboratories, where new colours were being created out of basic tones, and an increasing number of hues were being produced to achieve thousands and thousands of new colours.

Parallel to this artistic and technical evolution, the company was growing, expanding and becomig increasingly complex. At the end of the fifties, the Lladró brothers had opened a shop in the city of Valencia, and soon afterwards, two more shops were started up. These shops not only helped them to sell their creations, but also enabled them to keep up to date on new trends and on market demands, since the shops were dedicated to giftware in general.

"In a period of four to five years," added Juan, "we grew to about thirty people in the workshop we had at our parents' home. As soon as we had enough money, we set up shop in an old factory which we expanded a total of seven times in that decade. As it was, we did the planning ourselves in a uniform way, so even today it looks like it was simply one big factory bay."

In the late fifties, Lladró opened its first shop in Valencia. Shown below is a view of the opening ceremony. On the following page is "Two Women with Flagons", a creation dating from 1969. The elongated shapes, characteristic of many Lladró works during the sixties, form part of the stamp of the Lladró style which soon became popular at home and abroad.

The fabulous dynamics that Lladró enjoyed throughout the sixties was brought about by two key factors: the progressive internationalization of Lladró porcelain, and the start up of a school for professional training within the company.

ADVANCED MANAGEMENT TECHNIQUES

Jose Lladró remembers this time as one of the decisive moments of their career: "Coinciding with the start of the third enlargement of our first factory, in 1962, we opened our Professional Training School. We were conscious of how important it had been for us to learn how to mould and draw and practise composition and ceramic decoration under our teachers. Those studies had been so important for us, they had helped to mould us as persons and as artists, and we wanted to transmit this sensitivity and this experience to other people who had begun to work at our sides. It was also a way to make them better able to understand the spirit of what we were doing. Unlike us, our employees would not have to leave their workplaces and travel as far to get their training. We gave them lessons at the factory itself, during their working day.

Lladró has always been more than just a company. In the photo here, the three brothers joined forces with various employees to form their own soccer team.

After about half a year they began to appreciate the results. In those days it was difficult to find people who could draw and paint, and our school made up for the lack of artistic development among the population at large."

"The school was possible, among other reasons, thanks to the assistance of professor González Martí, founder of the National Ceramics Museum in Valencia that bears his name. He was a man of great prestige in his day. It was an honour to meet him and work with him. When we commented on our idea of founding a school, he told us that the Count of Aranda had the same idea when he started up his prestigious Alcora porcelain factory. When the authorization finally appeared in the Official State Gazette, after many trials and tribulations, a comment was included to the effect that such a school was 'exemplary and worthy of praise'. We eventually had thirty students enrolled at the school. Everyone who joined the company passed through the school, in fact. In a very short time, Lladró had a thirty-year head-start on staff training systems and consequently on production capacity."

Above, José and Juan with a group of physically handicapped Lladró employees. Below, cooking classes being given at the City of Porcelain.

One of the major aims of the Lladró brothers was to achieve a perfect integration of staff within the company. To do so, it was vital for them to aid employees in finding solutions to all their daily concerns, not simply job-related affairs. Company concerns therefore extended to employees' personal and family life, benefiting their entire families – husbands, wives, children and even parents. The company even provided support for hospitalization in case of need, and other services such as transport, travel arrangements, summer training courses, or the use of the sports complex for either leisure or as a part of company team activities. Swimming and sports events were organized for all. These and many other details confirm the Lladró

brothers' social involvement, with particular concern being given to the physically handicapped.

Midway through 1968 a local charity organization launched a newspaper campaign to encourage businessmen to show greater concern for the handicapped. A series of articles described how many physically handicapped persons are perfectly capable of dealing with normal jobs. This call to solidarity was enough to mobilize the efforts of the three brothers, who soon began including the physically handicapped in their staff selection process. They were trained just like any other operator, with the same rights and the same obligations, with the exception that facilities were

Free time activities for employees have always been promoted by Lladró.

provided to help them overcome their physical limitations.

In this way, despite suffering from physical handicaps, many local people were able to experience a feeling of joy at seeing their hopes and dreams come true, demonstrating that they were perfectly capable of doing creative work. Today, as many as sixty disabled people have managed to become part of the Lladró brothers' staff, encouraged by their will to succeed and the support of the company. They are fully integrated in company employment schemes and social activities. Some of them have even been able to form a family thanks to the personal relations they have made while working for Lladró.

This humanistic air which sets the tone at the company created by Juan, José and Vicente shows itself in many ways, and has been noted by outsiders on many occasions. On the professional level, it is easy to see how artistic talent and skills are brought to the fore at Lladró, as are consideration and respect for others, using non-authoritative management techniques. For example, at Lladró mistakes and errors made by employees have never been a cause for punitive action. Of course, managers do not let them go unnoticed; on the contrary what they do is meet with those involved to discuss the situation that gave rise to the errors and try to correct them, thereby helping all concerned to learn from a mistake. In many difficult areas of management, such as showing respect for others, integrating all employees in a shared project, incentivizing personal initiative, or promoting innovation, the Lladró brothers have done an extraordinary job.

Another highly important aspect in the company's human resources policies is the way its artists are trained – vital to Lladró's ongoing success. New artists are trained at the company's own scholarship centre, where they are carefully initiated into the Lladró philosophy and schooled in productive techniques. At a time when academic training underemphasizes realism, Lladró trains its own sculptors in the naturalistic tradition, thereby maintaining quality levels in the design process at the top of the yardstick, as well as simultaneously addressing innovation and continuity with skill and experience.

José Lladró with the Mateo sisters and other employees. Despite their physical handicaps, these veteran workers became fully integrated in the teams working at the City of Porcelain.

A FRUITFUL RELATIONSHIP.

González Martí will always be remembered as the founder of the National Museum of Ceramics of Valencia. This well-known institution is described in the chapter dedicated to Lladró figurines in world museums. There was always a close and fruitful relationship between this Valencian scholar, interested in artistic and craft traditions in the region, and the three Lladró brothers. Following the death of González Martí, Lladró has continued to collaborate with the museum that bears his name, as shown, for example, in its recent restoration of the Ballroom.

Below, González Martí's letter of thanks to the Lladró brothers, showing the great friendship between them and the Valencian scholar.

Two details from the ballroom of the Palace of the Marquis of Dos Aguas, headquarters of the González Martí National Museum of Ceramics restored under the patronage of Lladró.

SOCIAL EVENTS AND ART. As Lladró became an increasingly larger company with a growing number of employees, the three brothers were concerned to create an atmosphere in which relationships went beyond work to include free time and social events. In this way, the City of Porcelain was the stage for many other activities in addition to the daily work in the studios and laboratories – sports events, educational activities and cultural affairs were all part of the picture at a time when these services were unusual.
Above, the City of Porcelain celebrates Fallas. Below, the Lladró Women's Chorus.

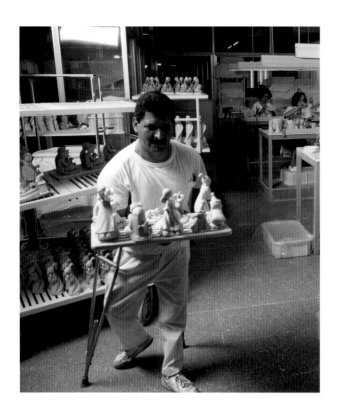 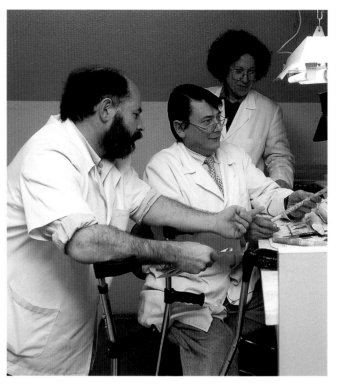

BEING ABLE. Another important area in which Lladró was a pioneer in Spain was the incorporation of people with physical handicaps into workplaces at the City of Porcelain. This experience has proven to be highly satisfactory, permitting the integration of many handicapped people in the working world and giving them the opportunity to develop their skills and abilities on both a social and professional level. Although handicapped, these people were able to take advantage of this opportunity and today are excellent professionals on the job, providing the company with essential skills and knowledge, and in some cases even becoming outstanding employees. The integration of the physically handicapped in the life of the City of Porcelain has extended to other areas as well. One example of this is the wheelchair basketball team composed of a group of Lladró workers who, thanks to their willpower and enthusiasm, have won a number of international trophies.

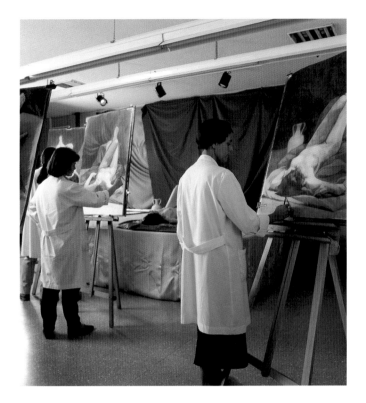

THE FASHIONING OF AN ARTIST. Becoming a part of the prestigious team of Lladró creators is the dream of many young artists. But this is a difficult achievement, because becoming a 'Lladró' artist requires talent, time and lots of effort. In order to find new talent in the field of porcelain art, the Lladró brothers decided to set up their own scholarship centre for young artists in training. From here, some may go on to become part of the team of sculptors working in the City of Porcelain. Students in the scholarship programme receive complete artistic training – drawing, modelling, anatomy, art history, ornamentation, etc. – and are taught by a team of professors and artists. Throughout their training period, these future artists have the chance to increase their professional qualifications, and absorb the special creative spirit pervading the Lladró studios.

While reminiscing about the internationalization process of the company, which began in the 1960s, José Lladró started by saying:

"In those days a group of Americans came to Valencia in search of decorative articles to import to their country. I remember showing them one of our pieces, a shepherd girl, that already had all the typical features of Lladró porcelain, with the colours we use today as well as our elongated style. As soon as they saw it they said they liked it. Among these Americans was Stanley Nagler."

As for Mr. Nagler, Vicente added:

"He loved our work. He tried to sell his company to us and stick with us. He was very enthusiastic about our products – at times he seemed like a fourth Lladró brother. He accompanied us to trade events and transmitted his love of porcelain to English-speaking buyers. He even bought a house near Valencia and spent long periods with us here, not only to work side by side with us, but also to take part in all our celebrations, frequently giving gifts to our employees. Later, just as he had promised, he made sure that everything was ready for us to buy out his company. It was a stroke of luck that we met this man with a distribution network already set

Three Lives, One Path

OPENING NEW AVENUES

Close association between the Lladró family and Stanley Nagler was fundamental to launching Lladró on the American market. In the photo below, Mr. Nagler is third from the left, seated between José Lladró's wife Carmen Castelló, and Vicente's wife Amparo Roig.

up in the United States. This structure, which was still modest in comparison to today, was the foundation on which we constructed our current market presence in that country."

In 1965 Lladró was exporting part of its works to Canada and was getting acquainted with the American market, which was still in the hands of Mr. Nagler. In 1969, the Lladró brothers made their first visit to America. The following year they attended their first international trade event in Hannover, Germany, and then took their creations to Sweden, Denmark and England, as well as to other important fairs such as the one in

Juan Lladró receives the "Export Leader" trophy in 1974. Lladró works were beginning to make a name for themselves outside Spain.

Cannes, France. It was a hectic time. Increasing export activities called for lots of hard work and continual adaptation to the challenges posed by these ventures into new markets. But it was also a time that gave the Lladró brothers great satisfaction. Not only did their products enjoy ever-growing popularity, but their circle of friends and admirers widened around the world. Many of the dealers with whom they established relationships in those days are still collaborating with Lladró today.

Lladró's newly won friends were not simply agents who considered their products to be outstanding sales articles. They were people from all around the world, from all kinds of backgrounds and walks of life, who appreciated style and artistry; it was a kindred feeling that brought all these people together, opening up new frontiers with every new year.

THE LLADRÓ CENTER IN NEW YORK. This building, located on 57th Street in Manhattan, contains the Lladró store, the headquarters of the Lladró Society in the United States, and a museum with the largest collection of Lladró pieces in the world, including a number of works created during the Lladró brothers' initial years.

VALENCIA

A NAME RECOGNIZED THROUGHOUT THE WORLD. Lladró has created a network of proprietary stores which includes Centres located in some of the most prestigious shopping and commercial areas in the world's leading cities. These centres offer the public a range of Lladró creations displayed in carefully arranged ambiences that highlight the artistic value of each piece.

Valencia, Madrid, London, New York, Beverly Hills, Singapore, Hong Kong... Lladró centres are important showcases for all the creations made by artists at the City of Porcelain, Spain.

LONDON

MADRID

HONG KONG

SINGAPORE

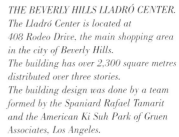

THE BEVERLY HILLS LLADRÓ CENTER.
The Lladró Center is located at
408 Rodeo Drive, the main shopping area
in the city of Beverly Hills.
The building has over 2,300 square metres
distributed over three stories.
The building design was done by a team
formed by the Spaniard Rafael Tamarit
and the American Ki Suh Park of Gruen
Associates, Los Angeles.

Lladró's venture into foreign markets started to fuel company growth. This growth was to become surprising and even spectacular over the following two decades. Some of the keys to this rapid and progressive development were certainly unusual: they were due more to a certain way of looking at life than to criteria of a purely corporate nature. As José explains:

THE KEY TO SUCCESS

"In the first place, we should highlight our studious and research-oriented focus. We have always been anxious to discover new things, to open up new horizons. Then we have to bear in mind the economic difficulties we faced when we were young, which forced us to work hard to rise up out of our poor and humble origins. We were trained under pressure, working eight to nine hours while dedicating an additional six or seven to our education.

In the second place, we have always felt a great commitment to society in the widest possible sense. Ever since our inception, lots of people have

José, Juan and Vicente during a celebration with Lladró employees.

wanted to work with us, people who were anxious to work, to make a future for themselves, many of them with lots of artistic sensitivity. In a way, we acted as their mentors, and by our side they learned their trade. Therefore we helped many people in our immediate area to increase their standard of living. We were faced with increasing demands for our products. It was not only that we fostered a desire for success, but rather the public simply kept on asking for more quality artworks from us. We have always responded to this situation in a responsible manner, that is, we have not simply acted from a selfish standpoint, moved by an ambition to create an ever-larger corporation. No, we were motivated largely by our circumstances, pushed forward by our willingness to serve and give service."

As anyone who has worked with them can confirm, the Lladró brothers have been successful in approaching their professional activities from the standpoint of maintaining their own personal taste, their will to outdo themselves and a high degree of commitment with the people who work with them, with whom they have always shared the same values and beliefs.

The '25 Years with Lladró' celebration paid respect to all those who had participated with the Lladró brothers in their personal and professional quest for over a quarter of a century.

Juan and José Lladró carefully inspect a figurine's decoration with Julio Ruiz.

They pride themselves on having triumphed thanks to the people who have helped them, although to be fair, the Lladró brothers possess qualities which were equally decisive in their success: prudence, ability and innocence... As it has been very appropriately pointed out, they are like the basic components of their porcelain, the raw material used in their creations: kaolin, feldspar and quartz – one provides the consistency, the other the plasticity and the third the hardness, and in combination they provide a product with extraordinary qualities indeed.

The success of Lladró lies in the warmth and trust they have always extended to the people they meet and work with. They have shown great skill in taking risks and dealing with difficult circumstances. They have been brave and innovative and have demonstrated the intuition required to create highly popular works of art with a personality of their own. They know how to recognize and value the feelings that people really care about and how to incorporate them in their figurines.

Left, Vicente Lladró with sculptor Salvador Debón. Below, José supervising the work done by a craftswoman.

Circumstances so combined to enhance their success. Spanish society was in the process of reconstruction and the Lladró brothers were able to meet the needs of this newborn society that wanted to give their homes greater warmth by decorating them with harmonious products showing beauty and sentiment. Later, other countries, having already recovered from the effects of war, also discovered this same beauty. And it was this recognition from outside Spain that reinforced the Lladró brothers' determination to continue their efforts to make their family project grow.

These are opinions which are shared by all those who continue to work side by side with the Lladró family, with the founding brothers and the members of the second generation who have joined their destinies to that of their parents. This was succinctly reflected in a speech given on behalf of all Lladró employees, at a ceremony paying homage to the founding brothers staged at the initiative of all staff members:

"... Don Juan, Don José and Don Vicente, we wanted to have you with us today, accompanied by your wives, to have the honour of personally expressing our acknowledgment of your long-standing and intense business activities during which you have been able to build a forward-looking company on solid foundations.

On the previous page, above, a monument in the City of Porcelain, erected at the initiative of the Lladró workers in homage to Juan, José and Vicente, the founders of the company. The inscription reads: "Your union is our future". Below, the Lladró brothers with their wives accepting the warm tribute of the staff. Above these lines, his Majesty King Juan Carlos with the Lladró brothers.

Becoming leaders in the field of porcelain art is a milestone that we passed some time ago, and although it was difficult to achieve this, it has been even more difficult to become a model corporation for so many different businesses in all sectors of the economy. Yet Lladró is recognized as such by countless VIPs in countries around the world.

All this is due to the quality and prestige you have achieved, and above all by your charisma and the family atmosphere you have been able to create and preserve over the years.

It should come as no surprise, therefore, to know that so many people have wanted and still want to become part of our company.

There are times of economic difficulty during which we all suffer setbacks, and against which we should all struggle to overcome with courage and stamina. It is at times like these when companies which are truly great show that they are able to withstand the onslaught of destiny and stand taller than many others. It is the 'savoir faire', the 'savoir faire bien' that brings success, breaks down all the barriers and opens the doors to the future.

Our future includes all of us, together, but also our children, the new generation – those young people who are sure to enrich our artistic skills and our human potential."

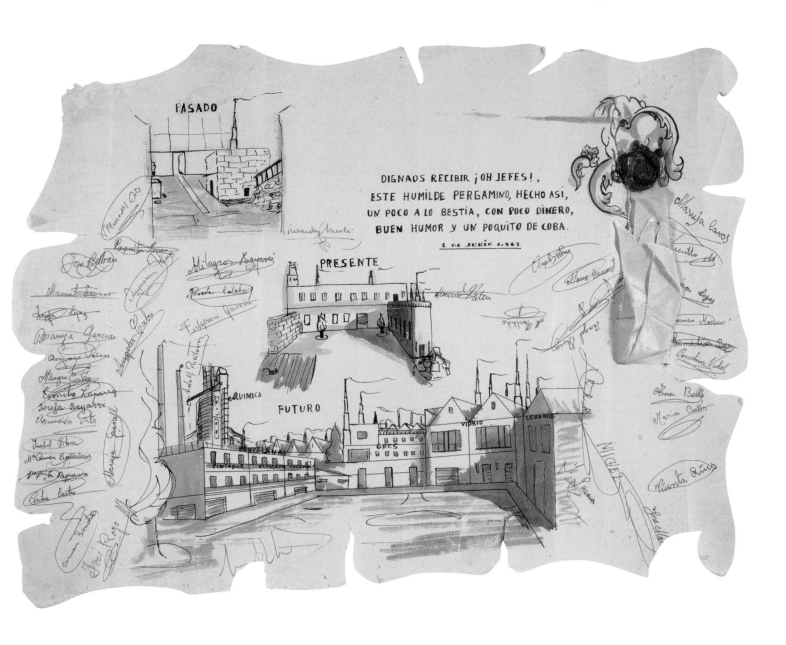

HOPES FOR THE FUTURE. This "humble parchment", as its authors jokingly call it, is a document showing the kind of 'family' atmosphere that has always been part of the Lladró studios. Also evident are the hopes and dreams of a series of workers who see the company as a project in which they are actively involved. This remembrance from the past was drawn by employees in 1961, and dedicated to the three brothers, includes the signatures of the people who worked with them. It illustrates the past, present and future of the firm. The past is shown top left, represented by the small kiln built in the patio of their parents' home, whereas the present, centre, portrays the installations commanded by a modest yet growing company. The most significant part of the document is the premonition of the future shown at the bottom of the parchment, anticipating what the City of Porcelain would become. It is a drawing of a large complex comprising workshops, warehouses and laboratories – a dream that enthusiastic employees would soon see coming true. In fact, the reality of the City of Porcelain surpassed their most optimistic dreams.

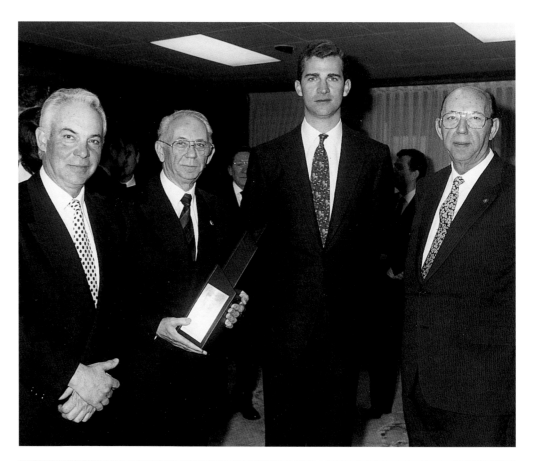

Above, the Lladró brothers with His Majesty Prince Felipe at the Business Excellence awards ceremony which bears his name. Lladró has won these awards on two occasions: in 1993 in the section devoted to Internationalization and in 1996 for Competitiveness.
On the right, the Lladró brothers with George Bush, the then vice-president of the United States.
On the next page, Juan Lladró and his wife, Dolores Sala at the reception held in Zarzuela Palace by Their Majesties the King and Queen of Spain for Their Excellencies the Emperors of Japan.
The following double page, three generations of the family at a private audience granted by His Holiness John Paul II.

The opening of a new Lladró Center on Rodeo Drive in March 1997 was the event of the week in Los Angeles. It brought together over 400 celebrities and VIPs from the field of politics, culture, and the arts. Top, Lauren Bacall with the Lladró brothers and Carmen Castelló de Lladró. Left, Rosa Lladró Sala with Tippi Hedren and Janet Leigh. Right, Vicente Lladró, actress Loni Anderson, José Lladró, Peggy Goldwyn, Samuel Goldwyn Jr.'s wife, and Juan Lladró.

Top, Dolores Sala de Lladró, Juan Lladró, Michael Douglas, Edie Wasserman, wife of Lew Wasserman of MCA Universal, and Janet Leigh.
Left, Amparo Roig de Lladró, her son Juan Vicente Lladró, actor Charlton Heston, and his wife Lydia.
Right, actor Michael York and his wife with Rosa María Lladró.

MANKIND'S DREAM. *During a visit to the Vatican, José, on behalf of the entire Lladró family and staff, offered the Three Kings to his Holiness Pope Paul VI as a present. A few years later one of mankind's age-long dreams came true when the first man stepped onto the moon. The three-man crew of the Apollo XI moon mission, Armstrong, Aldrin and Collins, were given an audience by the Pope while touring the world after this feat, and during their interview they received from His Holiness a significant gift – the Three Kings originally from the City of Porcelain.*

In 1994, to commemorate the 25th anniversary of this feat, Lladró created a piece called "The Apollo Landing" to pay tribute to the men who had made mankind's dream come true.

In the ceremony held at the Lladró Center in New York, José Lladró unveiled "The Apollo Landing". Attending the event was Buzz Aldrin, one of the Apollo XI crew members, who pronounced these heartfelt words: "When Pope Paul VI presented us with Lladró's the Three Kings, he spoke of a mission 2,000 years ago. A mission by three men who were guided by the stars so they might carry a message to all mankind. His allegorical reference to our mission touched us deeply."

Below left, José Lladró giving Pope Paul VI the Three Kings and right, His Holiness handing the same figurine to one of the crew members of Apollo XI some years later.

Above left, José Lladró presents "The Apollo Landing" to Buzz Aldrin, a crewmember of the mission that finally reached the moon on that historic day of July 20th 1969. Lladró commemorated the 25th anniversary of this feat by creating the piece shown above right. Below right, a photograph dedicated to the Lladró family, of Aldrin's first walk on the moon.

Over the years the founding brothers overcame many difficulties and crucial moments. They did so with a sense of responsibility, with their customary good humour and their brotherly love inspired and fostered by their mother. New sculptors entered the team, new product lines were launched such as Gres, Sculptures and Caprichos. Creation procedures were perfected in the search for greater quality and enhanced beauty. New creations were born and Lladró workers and artists increased to meet the new demands of having entered new markets. The family workshop grew to acquire the dimensions of a small city dedicated to the world of art, which sometimes created problems derived mostly from rapid growth and the increasing complexity of their business structures. But over four decades of unflagging efforts they have also accumulated countless gratifying experiences and obtained the rewards of knowing that they have lived good lives. They are appreciated by millions of people throughout the world, and it is a satisfaction for them to have created works which are loved and valued by people from all walks of life and from practically every cultural grouping in the world.

Three Lives, One Path

TAKING STOCK OF A LIFETIME

Of all the satisfactions that life has given to the Lladró brothers, perhaps one of the greatest is knowing that they have created works which are appreciated and admired by art lovers the world over. Shown below and on the following page is "Tea in the Garden".

"Our pieces show tenderness, sensitivity, spirituality; they enrapture people at first sight. It is not we who say so – it is a fact that we have witnessed thousands of times. Sometimes when people shake our hands they look at them incredulously as if to say 'are these really the hands that make such beautiful works of art?' At times one feels almost embarrassed by such situations," confesses Vicente.

José remembers other similar occurrences:

"On one occasion, a lady walked up to one of our sculptures while a modelling demonstration was being given in a shop in Indonesia, and she said she believed that we were good people because if we could make pieces like that we simply had to be good. What she wanted to express were the feelings she had upon seeing the tenderness and sensitivity of a sculpture that was being created before her very eyes. And the truth is that whether or not that comment was exaggerated, at Lladró we do try to transmit warmth, humanity, and a positive way of looking at life."

Of all the kudos and recognition, what the founding brothers most value is without a doubt the fact that so many people have stood by their side over the years, helping them to progress along the road to success. As Juan Lladró once said at a get-together called '25 Years with Lladró' held to commemorate a group of employees' first quarter of a century at the company:

"We have worked hard, shoulder to shoulder, and all those efforts have made it possible for us to say that there is a Lladró figurine in practically every corner of the world. But the most important thought is that in each of those pieces, which belong to all of you, which were made by all of us, there is joy, sentiment, love. We send messages of love and peace out into the world, and this is undoubtedly what the world needs most."

At each new meeting with porcelain art lovers around the world, wherever they happen to be, the Lladrós are able to confirm just how much their works are welcomed and appreciated, despite geo-

The Lladró brothers have had the satisfaction of seeing how their creations are loved and admired by people of all ages, nationalities and cultures.

The Lladró Board.

graphical distance and cultural differences. It is a unique experience which the new generation of the family has been able to enjoy in recent years, as the younger members of the three founding brothers' families take up new responsibilities within the company. The members of the new generation have all grown up in a family that considers porcelain art as a way of life, completing their education by working within the company so that they can gain firsthand knowledge of the creations that bear their names, and become fully integrated in company management circles.

At present, the new generation plays an active role in the figurine creation process and in many events of a social nature, infusing new life and skills in the tradition founded by their parents. Among other activities, they perform a duty that they think is one of the most gratifying of all, that of representing Lladró at events and meetings attended by the public.

Guaranteeing the continuity of their work was one of the first concerns of the Lladró brothers. Their approach to this challenge was to conceive the future of the company as a projection of their past experience, with an outlook stressing ongoing progress intended to foster all initiatives that might help the company in its advance. This approach involved emphasizing the artistic and personal values that had served them so well in the past. From a very young age, they began to delegate responsibilities to the people who are inexorably called upon to carry on their work – their children, the direct heirs of their legacy.

On January 20th 1984 the Lladró brothers opened the doors to the future by allowing three of their children to enter management circles in the company – one child from each of the founding brothers. They joined the Lladró Board, and took on jobs involving a great deal of responsibility within the company, including those related to the creativity committee. This brought about a long and intense process whereby knowledge was passed from father to son, or

Three Lives, One Path

PASSING ON A FAMILY TRADITION

from father to daughter. Rosa, Mari Carmen and Juan Vicente underwent the difficult task of learning everything they could about the unique company founded by their parents and the way it operated.

The way the Lladró brothers approached the delicate issue of succession was based on non-coercive methods. It is only natural that some descendants should show an interest and inclination towards the work of their parents, whereas others should possess some other talents. The founding brothers have always respected these differences in their families. For this reason, the gateway to Lladró has always been open to members of the second generation who were able to demonstrate the necessary aptitudes and will to make the effort to acquire responsibility within the company. These requirements are no different from those that must be demonstrated by any other employee. Members of the second generation work side by side with their elders in both everyday business tasks and the delicate job of channelling creativity. On the one hand they must be adept at managing the company resources they may have under their control, both human and technical, and on the other hand

Three members of the second Lladró generation have taken over from their parents at the head of the company: from left to right, Rosa, Mari Carmen and Juan Vicente.

they have to know the artistic secrets which are at the heart of Lladró porcelain figurines. Along the way they have been helped not only by the invaluable advice of their parents, but also by the excellent team of employees trained directly by the Lladró brothers over many years. These people are also key elements in assuring the continuity of the company, like cells permanently regenerating the fabric of the corporation, keeping it ready for operation at all times. The members of the second generation of porcelain-creating Lladrós are fully aware of all this, which is why they have always been involved in the company from their earliest opportunity, learning step by step how porcelain figurines are created – from the time they first take shape under the skilled hands of the sculptor, until the fire of the kilns gives them their peculiar crystalline textures and highlights their beautiful pastel colours for all to see.

Throughout the process of transmitting values, the art lover is always present, because it is the admirer of Lladró art who is the object of all company efforts, the source of inspiration for universal works that touch people's hearts everywhere, answering aspirations and reflecting the noblest of desires.

The Lladró family's second generation represents the present and the future of a family dedicated in body and soul to porcelain art.

The City of Porcelain is located in unusual surroundings, where the Valencian 'huerta' (market gardens and orchards) intermeshes with the town forming a puzzle-like landscape in which modern buildings and communications networks contrast sharply with the traditional market gardens cultivated since antiquity in this region. Leaving the city of Valencia northwards, we come off the motorway and drive along country roads, running beside irrigation channels and reedbeds, between orange orchards and artichoke fields, flanked by porches overgrown with centuries-old grapevines.

2. A DAY IN THE LIFE OF THE CITY OF PORCELAIN

The visitor is approaching the land where Lladró porcelain was born, and senses that the journey is nearing its end when the signpost marks the limits of Tavernes Blanques, where a large complex can be seen in the distance. At the entrance, there is a group of sculptures acting as fountainpieces, and a plaque bears the inscription: "Lladró, Ciudad de la Porcelana". After crossing the threshold, the new guest enters a broad expanse of land with wide avenues set between luxuriant gardens. In the foreground is an Olympic size swimming pool and other sports facilities set in the middle of the complex, around which a number of buildings are arranged symmetrically.

Life within the City of Porcelain flows smoothly, with that special kind of rhythm that characterizes the work of artists.

The City of Porcelain is a peaceful, practical place. When it was first designed in the 1960s, everything was arranged with the idea that people should work in surroundings which develop and perfect their artistic skills, while enabling them to have spare time for sports and leisure activities. The three founding brothers envisaged a site that would ideally suit both them and their artists, a complex that would inspire creativity and contribute to painstaking artisanship. And this is what they have achieved.

A PLACE FOR CREATION

The first phase was begun on November 2nd 1967, and it was finished in less than two years. On October 13th 1969 the Minister of Industry, Gregorio López Bravo, cut the ribbon on the first installations in the complex. These were later successively enlarged to meet increasing demands for space.

Strolling along the avenues, the visitor discovers a carefully laid-out arrangement in which the location and style of the buildings are in harmony with their surroundings. The layout is functional yet pleasing to the eye, fostering efficiency with equal concern for beauty.

At the City of Porcelain there is a pleasing mixture of buildings and facilities intended for both work and leisure.

One unusual construction stands out from the rest because of its original design. It looks like a pyramid, and houses the sculptors' studios, where all Lladró creations are brought to life.

Here, artists and sculptors spend long hours giving shape to each and every piece in the Lladró repertoire. Some model original pieces in clay, some are specialists who study the procedures used to make replicas of original moulds in fine porcelain, while others are solely concerned with the decoration to be applied on completed figurines.

Inside this building there is a special kind of atmosphere. An almost monastic silence reigns supreme, making the visitor feel that he or she is entering a secret realm, created to provide artists with the ideal environment for inspiration and the outflow of creativity. The pyramid provides lots of light – intense Mediterranean light – that permeates the spacious studios, where some of the greatest works created by Lladró sculptors can still be seen.

The first floor houses the sculptors' studios, arranged around a cloister-like central patio. They all look very similar. They are the same size, they have the same furnishings, they are crowned by the same skylights. Nevertheless, within their architectural unity, each studio shows the personality of the artists working here, noticeable in the decoration, the details, the music being played, the arrangement of the tools and working instruments.

On the shelves, cluttered with rough black-and-white sketches in various stages of completion, we may recognize a Lladró figurine in any of its various stages prior to completion. The clay figure always looks suggestive and evocative, going back as it does to the primeval beginnings of creation. When faced with a clay form, we usually ask ourselves how a Lladró figurine is actually created, where its inspiration comes from, what idea moves the sculptor to give physical shape to an image in the mind's eye.

The answer can be found within the walls of this building, in the intimate artistic relationship that exists between the Lladrós and their team of sculptors. Ever since the three founding brothers decided to unite their talents in the forties, this relationship with their artists has been intense and fruitful.

The Lladró brothers have played the master to men of mastery, they have been mentors to disciples who have become inspired artists, guiding the steps of many talented people who have joined the staff. While progressing together along the road to porcelain art, there has been a mutual intermingling of experiences and talents, and everyone has reached such a degree of understanding that sometimes it is impossible to discover who is the true creator of a piece. Everyone shares the same sources of inspiration, the same artistic concerns, the same means of expression, and their creations are born into that special atmosphere we can sense in the City of Porcelain.

In a way, this 20th-century artists' studio has an air much like the studios of Renaissance artists in which skills and knowledge were passed on from masters to disciples through intense and enriching personal relationships.

The sculptors' studio, designed by Rafael Tamarit, is one of the most spectacular buildings in the City of Porcelain. Here, every day, Lladró artists take pains to give life to new creations destined to reach every corner of the globe.

Between the Lladró family and their sculptors there is a kind of artistic affinity that facilitates communication. Ever since the three founders decided to join forces in the forties, their relationship with artists has been close and productive.

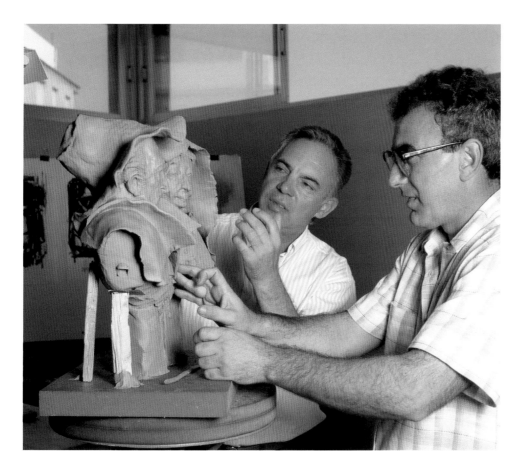

The Lladró brothers, as artists and art patrons at the same time, have transferred this spirit from their studios to the classroom by creating their own
training centres. Close to the sculptors' studio is the Lladró Scholarship
Centre, where young aspiring artists learn to develop their talents. They are
would-be sculptors and designers who have come to the City of Porcelain only
after passing rigorous selection exams, and they all share one common dream
which will only come true for a few of them – that of working with the Lladró
family to give life to new figurines.

Each Lladró figurine is the result of a fascinating yet complex process
which Lladró family members supervise carefully, step by step. Based on an
original idea whose inspiration is taken from the history of art, from nature, or
from day-to-day life, a Lladró sculptor makes an initial mockup of a figurine in
clay. This rough sculpture has to pass its first difficult test: a rigorous examina-
tion by the Lladró family. Once it has been approved, the sculptor re-models it in
full detail and to its proper scale, bearing in mind the reduction it will experience during firing. When completed, the prototype is transferred to the technical

department, where it is painstakingly sliced into a series of segments, and these separate pieces are then moulded in alabaster or plaster of Paris. All the parts are then reassembled to obtain an exact reproduction. The result is a model that goes back to the original sculptor, who defines all the finer details to be incorporated into this piece. The prototype is then sent to the ornamentation department, where specialists decorate it following the indications of the sculptor. Here, delicate details are engraved over the smooth surface of the piece to give it a lifelike appearance.

Above, a sculptor models a piece in clay. Below, the prototype is carefully cut into segments which will be reproduced in alabaster or plaster of Paris for mould making (next page).

Sculptors and artists are linked by mutual understanding and an intuitive grasp of their work. Everything depends on this vital form of artistic communication, because figurine decorators have the difficult task of completing a job initiated by others.

Men and women working in this department come from the Faculty of Fine Arts, from the Lladró Scholarship Centre, or have attended the San Carlos School of Arts and Crafts in Valencia – the same institution where

the Lladró brothers themselves were trained half a century ago. Some of the artists have classical training, some are self-taught, but all are excellent draughtsmen or draughtswomen.

Their task is painstaking and complicated. They have to get the feel of each creation. They must find that delicate kind of harmony which exists between the individual parts and the complete creation, between the ornamental and the expressive. They have to achieve a balanced result.

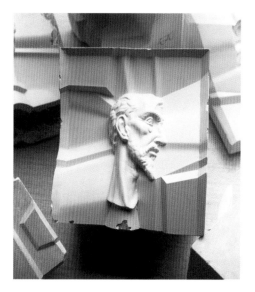 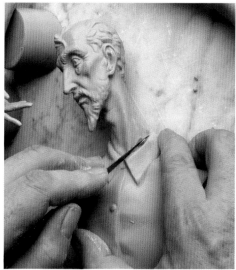

The decision concerning which motifs go on each piece is part of the sculptor's job, but the factors influencing the final result include shared ideas, documentation on the theme in question and creative imagination.

Once these tasks have been concluded, the piece is transported to a nearby building where it will have to pass rigorous tests before it can be sent to the workshops. Various prototypes in porcelain undergo a complete cre-

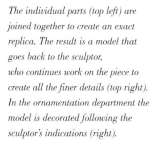

The individual parts (top left) are joined together to create an exact replica. The result is a model that goes back to the sculptor, who continues work on the piece to create all the finer details (top right). In the ornamentation department the model is decorated following the sculptor's indications (right).

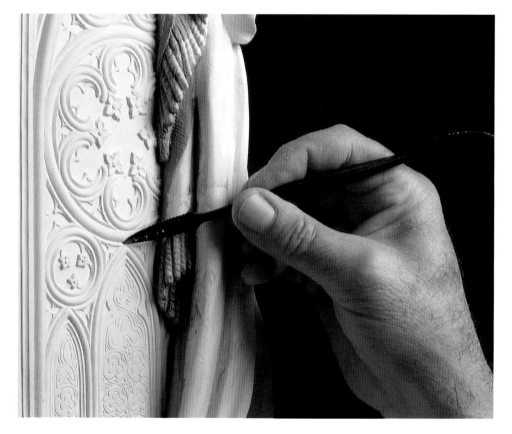

ation process until the figurine comes out of the kiln in perfect condition.

The artists who decorate each creation will test out a number of chromatic compositions using the extensive Lladró palette of colours that now includes over 4,000 hues. Finding the right combination for each figurine is an arduous task.

Throughout the entire creation process, prototypes normally undergo up to half a dozen modifications before being approved. There is an expression at Lladró to the effect that 'porcelain is alive', used particularly by the technical department to refer to the challenge of giving life to a new creation – a task undertaken by an entire team, from sculptors to technicians – with a material as difficult to master and as delicate as porcelain. In the kiln, where clay is transformed into precious porcelain, the flames subject each piece to the final test.

The process is labour-intensive and time-consuming. But eventually the moment comes when the figurine leaves the sculptors' studio and enters the workshops, ready to be made and sent to countries around the world.

The artists who decorate each piece test out a series of chromatic compositions before finding the one that best suits the figurine in question.

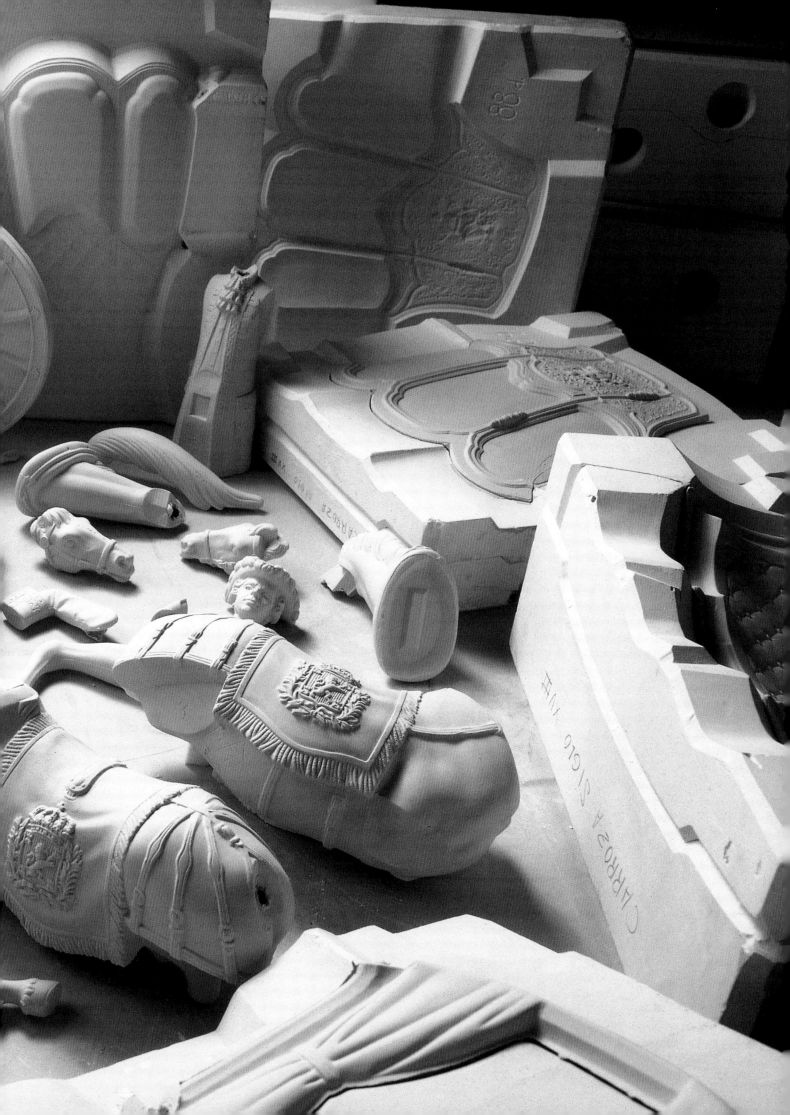

There is an underground network of liquid porcelain paste channels in the sub-soil of the City of Porcelain. This subterranean river flows into one of the most fascinating departments in the whole complex – the laboratory. Access is not open to the public because this section safe-guards one of the best kept secrets of Lladró, which is none other than the formula for making such fine porcelain. Kaolin, water, quartz and feldspar are the natural ingredients which are combined in exact proportions to provide a porcelain paste that flows through the pipelines to feed three buildings where figurines are made. In each of these liquid paste is used to fill the moulds, and this is how the figurine creation process is initiated.

CLAY, COLOUR AND FIRE

This job requires a great deal of concentration, and above all, years of skill and experience. The person in charge of mould filling has to be thoroughly familiar with the moulds: how to fill them without producing bubbles, how long it takes for the porcelain to harden in each particular mould, how to run off the excess water, where to begin opening each mould, and many other tasks.

After proper draining the moulds must be opened. This calls for a firm and gentle hand. As each piece of an individual figurine is extracted, the original sculpture comes back to life, but in piecemeal form. The artisan extracts each segment with care so as not to leave fingerprints on the tender porcelain. Then,

The laboratory, one of the most fascinating places in the City of Porcelain, is off limits to the public, as it contains one of the best guarded secrets of the Lladró company – the formula for making such fine porcelain.

with the same meticulous care, he or she proceeds with a mould cleaning operation to ensure that it can be reused for a certain number of times in perfect condition, until the limit is reached or the slightest sign of a defect is observed.

Each figurine may require as many as fifteen to twenty moulds, although some complicated compositions may be composed of up to two hundred different segments.

But let us take things step by step. We are in one of the moulding rooms, with countless fragments before us corresponding to different figurines waiting to be reassembled into a recognizable form. Following a humidification process to

ensure the right consistency, they are taken to a section where they are rebuilt using liquid porcelain paste that acts as an adhesive.

Until this time, the process is controlled by a limited number of people, but the reassembly procedure involves a large number of artisans – mostly women – who show great skill in carrying out the remaining steps in the procedure before the pieces are taken to the firing section. In different workshops, some women painstakingly reconstruct the pieces using segments given to them on trays. Others begin to paint different parts of each figurine, and the most skilled and experienced have the job of giving life to each porcelain face. Eyes, eyebrows, lips, a smile or a longing look are the masterworks of these expert decorators whose firm hands outline the expressions specified by the original sculptor under the supervision of the Lladró family.

Above, filling the moulds with liquid porcelain is a delicate task that requires lots of concentration. Below, each figurine needs an average of fifteen to twenty moulds, although some special compositions are made up of over two hundred individual segments.

Tables are full of paintbrushes and jars of ceramic hues. At first glance the colours contained in the jars do not correspond to the soft Lladró tones we know so well from art exhibitions and collections. Strange blue hair and purple lips are the initial result of some of these painters' work. But what we see here are the guide tones, used to facilitate the decorating process, and these colours will be burned off in the kiln before the true glazes flower on the surface of each piece.

After being fired in giant kilns at over 1,300°C (2,372°F) for practically one whole day, the

figurines still have to pass several important quality controls. This guarantees that all figurines leaving Porcelain City will be absolutely perfect, as accredited by the stamp engraved onto the base of each figurine, certifying its authenticity.

At the last stop on this imaginary tour of the Lladró studios, the visitor can see how figurines showing the slightest defect are destroyed on the spot during quality control inspections. After a close-up overview of the meticulous process undergone by each piece one cannot help but feel a pang of sadness at seeing an otherwise beautiful creation being shattered to pieces, above all

The individual segments of each figurine are joined together using liquid porcelain paste, which acts as an adhesive. Following this process, the figurine regains it original shape.

when the majority of 'defects' can only be detected by the trained eye of a specialist.

Nevertheless, there are few pieces that do not pass the quality controls, since they are so meticulously made. The majority of them are sent on to the packing area where they are manually fitted into boxes designed specifically for each individual figurine. From here, they will leave the City of Porcelain to travel to homes in over one hundred and fifty countries on all five continents of the globe.

The delicate flowers decorating many Lladró figurines and compositions are made one by one, petal by petal, thanks to the extraordinary skills of specialists (above). Artists are responsible for painting the figurines, but only the most experienced will give life to a figurine's face (right).

After being fired in Lladró kilns at a temperature above 1,300°C (2,372°F) for practically an entire day, the figurine presents its finished form.

When it comes out of the kiln, the figurine still has to pass a series of quality controls. If it presents even the slightest blemish or defect (above), it is mercilessly destroyed. Once it passes these controls, however, it is sent to the packaging department, where it is manually fitted into a box which is specially designed for each figurine (below).

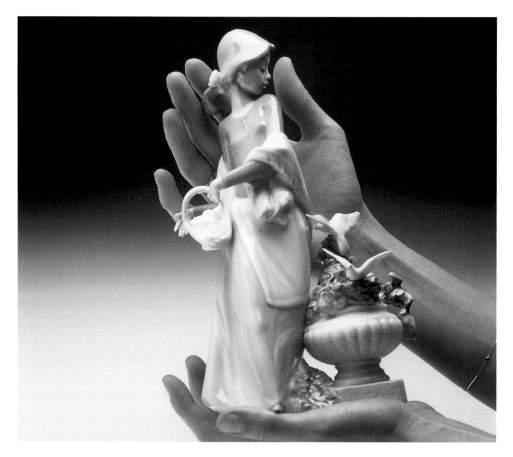

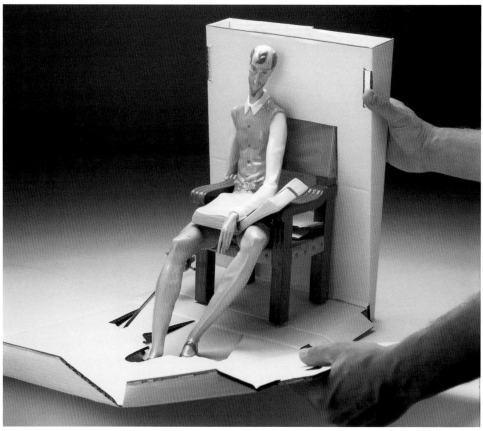

GRES

Juan Lladró

Gres is one of the materials we use at Lladró because of its extraordinary beauty and its expressive power.

The Spanish word "gres" is usually referred to in industry as stoneware, such as that used by manufacturers of floor tiles, who emphasize the strength and resistance of their stoneware, but never talk about its versatility. It is true that Gres is very strong, but this is only one of its multiple features.

The origin of Gres, like metal, goes back to the times of primitive man. Together with earthenware bowls and jars and pottery, we can find other ceramic materials that would be shown to contain metallic elements in their compositions if they were subjected to analysis. This is due to the larger or smaller amount of ferruginous materials in the different types of clay that were used, in the form of oxides, sulphates, carbonates, micas, illites and chlorites, among other materials. These all accelerate fusion, providing a higher resistance to breakage. The higher the firing temperature the greater the strength of the material produced, as long as the optimum firing temperature for each formula is reached but not exceeded.

With regard to the colouring of Gres, which depends on its exact composition, this ranges from white to grey including creams and tans, sometimes resulting in blues or greens, and extending all the way to dark anthracite and black. Gres does not have the transparency of porcelain, but we might say it has the same hardness. Its texture varies from a fine substance akin to porcelain up to granulated textures that look like rough refractory materials.

The use of Gres in the field of art is fully justified in that it provides materials full of beautiful nuances, easily perceptible to the naked eye and to our sense of touch, making Gres compositions subtle and rich. To decorate Gres pieces we use high-temperature ceramic glazes that often transmit colours and effects of great beauty.

We might say that porcelain is exquisite because of its purity and transparency, whereas Gres has the capacity to express the strength and power of the sophisticated artist.

The combination of Gres with earthy tones, glazes and crystallizations achieves highly sophisticated effects which are sometimes the product of caprice and chance.

Gres is therefore a noble material, worthy of the sensitive artist and the rigorous critic. This is why it forms part of the Lladró collection.

I hope this will give you a clearer vision of Gres. It was my intention to awaken your curiosity with respect to a material that has long been part of our culture. And I hope you will enjoy it and appreciate all its wonderful beauty.

THE MAGIC OF COLOUR

José Lladró

If we look at the work of Valencian artists, we can see that colour is a fundamental element in all their creations. The particularly intense Mediterranean light that shines in our region exerts a powerful influence over the way we see things and represent them in art. In my student days at the School of Arts and Crafts I was influenced by Sorolla, Benlliure and other Valencian painters whose works were full of vibrant colours, reflecting in an extraordinary way those rich nuances of the light we enjoy on the shores of the Mare Nostrum.

When I started work in the field of porcelain together with my brothers, our first works were decorated using bright colours following the classic European tradition. But our creations have always been characterized by a relentless search, and we soon began experimenting with firing techniques and pigments, looking for new ways to decorate our creations.

I remember discovering the attractions of grey tones one rainy day in winter. I had gone out into the country to paint a typical landscape of the Valencian 'huerta', a field known as 'Les Llengües'. I was impressed by the beauty of the grey wintertime sky that toned down the colours of the trees, the water, and the surrounding fields... I tried to transfer that delicate harmony onto my canvas, and later in the studio, I began experimenting with ways to reflect those colours on porcelain.

Not long afterwards, as I was examining a figurine of a deer being chased by hunting dogs, which was painted using colours which I thought a bit too bright, I decided to decorate another figurine following my personal inspiration. I used a range of grey, beige and soft brown tones. The results couldn't have been better, to my eyes. Since that time, we have been working hard to extend our ample palette of pigments and perfect the process of painting and firing our porcelain. I believe that the efforts involved were worthwhile. We achieved a new way of using colour which was perfectly adapted to the delicacy of porcelain, enabling us to enrich our works with an almost limitless range of chromatic combinations. And it has given us great satisfaction that all of you have acknowledged our efforts by opening your arms to our creations over all these years.

I think the true essence of Lladró porcelain lies in the balance it shows between form and colour. It is a delicate combination that can only be found in true works of art. On a recent trip I found a magnificent example in the main square of Prague, which in itself is a monumental architectural composition combining a rich palette of colours presented by the buildings in the square, all in extraordinary harmony. I believe the sensitivity of the creators of this marvellous square is very close to the kind we feel.

The history of sculpture, in which we find so many masterful monochrome works, shows just how complex it is to make a good decorated sculpture. Imagine, for example, how difficult it would be to colour Michelangelo's David. We who work at Lladró strive every day to make sure that our creations successfully pass the difficult test of finding the right chromatics.

TRIAL BY FIRE

Vicente Lladró

I was very young when my elder brothers started work as painters in a tile and dishware factory near our home town. Their talents soon led them to experiment and work to master ceramic techniques in the very little free time they had available— first in the factory itself, where the kiln operators did them the favour of firing their own creations at night, and later in the courtyard of the family home, where a bricklayer friend built a small kiln for firing bowls that we later had to rebuild because it didn't work properly.

When I joined forces with my brothers, I was attracted by that little kiln which was the torment of quite a few people in our neighbour- hood due to its penchant for belching out smoke at unearthly times.

It burnt fuel badly, whatever we did to it. Yet I was attracted above all by its power to create beauty and its power to destroy, seemingly of its own free will. It was frustrating to see how an excellent piece of workmanship would enter the kiln, only to come out wrong if something happened during firing, the last step in a long process. There was no other option but to go back to the beginning again, without knowing whether the next piece would ever see the light of day, because of the difficulties involved.

The temperature we finally achieved with this kiln only served to fire low-temperature ceramics, not porcelain, yet porcelain was our aim. We started by making flowers for a lamp manufacturing company, which sold them at three pesetas a piece or at six or seven pesetas for a group of three. All three of us modelled them; my brothers painted them and I was in charge of firing them. We fired in three stages: one for the clay, another for the glazes and a third firing for the colours.

With the first money we made, we decided to build a kiln capable of reaching higher temperatures. We had to rebuild the kiln various times before we finally managed to fire porcelain. Building it was not an easy job, as we used refractory bricks recovered from waste materials at the steel mills of Sagunto, and reconstructing the 'puzzle' of irregularly-shaped bricks we collected was a laborious and complicated task.

Achieving porcelain firing was undoubtedly the major breakthrough of our careers, the decisive step forward, because at last we were able to overcome the technical barrier that had prevented us from making true porcelain, that dreamed-of materi- al that would give body to our artistic feelings. The second step forward came in 1960 when we started single firing at high temperatures.

Since then, many years have passed, giving us time to do endless research and perfect our firing techniques, a process I have been closely involved with. Both my brothers and I, in our desire to outdo our own work again and again, made this achieve- ment thanks to the excellent team we gathered around us. Just as we innovated in design to style our figurines in our own way, we also introduced changes in certain departments, including the firing section, where we finally managed to do what we had formerly done in three firings in only one single journey to the kiln. Moreover, by doing so, we achieved the crys- talline finish and the pastel hues we are now so famous for.

Looking back today, I can still recall the smell of the gorse and rosemary we used to light the fire in our very first kiln, the one that produced such dense smoke. And, in a way, I miss that struggle at such close quarters with the roaring flames.

After touring the studios and workshops in which we were given a step-by-step explanation of the way Lladró figurines are made, one stops to contemplate and review what we have seen. By becoming familiar with all the details of this miraculous process repeated day in day out, we cannot help but feel impressed by the work that goes into each figurine – the creativity, the effort, the time and the skill.

A Day in the Life of the City of Porcelain

A COSMOPOLITAN CITY

Porcelain art lovers around the world are the ones who feel this fascination most deeply, and this explains why it is normal to find groups of visitors at the City of Porcelain at almost any time. They are people who come from virtually all over the world to gain a firsthand glimpse of the place where Lladró figurines are brought to life. Many of these people are members of the Lladró Society, which was created in 1985 and in just over a decade gained a membership of over 100,000 people who are self-declared admirers of Lladró art.

The Lladró Society is proud to include people of different nationalities and different backgrounds who have found that porcelain art is a passion they all share.

Among the privileges enjoyed by members of the Lladró Society is the possibility of making a visit to any of the Lladró museums or exhibition centres

The City of Porcelain is frequently visited by groups of people who come from many parts of the world to get a personal view of the place where Lladró figurines are made.

The Guest Book at the City of Porcelain has signatures from people as famous as Paul A. Samuelson, Norman Foster, the Duchess of Badajoz, Buzz Aldrin, Tippi Hedren, Raisa Gorbachova, Joaquín Cortés, Michael Jackson and the Nobel prizewinners Dr. Arber and Dr. Smith.

located around the world, and especially to the site where all figurines are made – the City of Porcelain in Spain – where they are always made welcome.

The chance to tour the City of Porcelain is particularly attractive for Lladró Society members. Many of them have long dreamed of visiting this sanctuary of porcelain art, and when they get home again, the visit makes them look at the pieces in their private collection with new understanding, and renewed joy. An overview of the City of Porcelain helps them to understand that each work is the fruit of the inspiration and sentiments of all the men and women who have contributed to its birth. Because of their talents, efforts and love, Lladró figurines come to life.

And once our guided tour of the figurine creation process comes to an end, there is still one building we should not miss. It is a building that contains some of the most frequented rooms in the entire City of Porcelain – the exhibition rooms, presenting a complete collection of current figurines, and the Elite Hall, in which all the most prestigious figurines created by Lladró for the Elite collection are on display. This build-

Lladró's exhibition room at the City of Porcelain is what probably touches visitors the most. To see all of Lladró's creations under one roof, displayed in an area of hundreds of square metres is something which many porcelain art lovers will never forget.

ing also preserves a part of the history of the City of Porcelain which very few are familiar with in its entirety – the Book of Honour. Within the pages of this book we can find the signatures and comments of a long list of renowned personalities and leading celebrities from the fields of politics, economics, the sciences and the arts. Among them is the signature of the architect Norman Foster; the Nobel Prizewinner in Economics, Paul A Samuelson; the Mayor of St. Petersburg, Anatoli Sobchak; Raisa Gorbachova; Michael Jackson; the Governor of Vatican City, Castillo Lara; the President of the Economic and Social Committee of the European Union, Carlos Ferrer Salut; the dancer Joaquín Cortés; and the American astronaut Buzz Aldrin.

All of these and many others have come to the tiny town of Tavernes Blanques in Valencia, Spain, moved by the desire to see the City of Porcelain and witness the figurine creation process accompanied by some exceptional hosts – none other than the Lladró brothers. Side by side they have strolled through the gardens, visited the studios, and have seen, for an hour or two, the complicated yet wonderful world of porcelain art at Lladró.

On our visit to the Lladró studios, we saw how Lladró figurines come to life, and we have also had the opportunity to share some time with the people who work in the City of Porcelain. During our tour we have been able to gain an understanding of the work that goes on within its walls, but we can also see that life in the City of Porcelain transcends labour-related aspects. At the City of Porcelain people work, and work hard, but they also study, do sports, and make friends...

SOCIAL LIFE

Around the entire complex social activities are underway. The Lladró brothers have always been concerned to see that their employees – apart from their obligations – have the chance to broaden their horizons and enjoy their free time to the full. As an example, people working at Lladró take English classes, computer classes, painting, university preparation courses, secondary school certificates and even childbirth preparation classes, cooking and tennis classes.

Visitors to the City of Porcelain are able to see how the work of Lladró artists is a combination of talent, dedication and sensitivity – three factors that help us to understand the true meaning of Lladró creations.

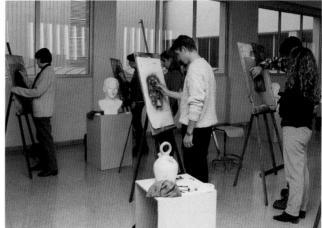

All kinds of healthcare is provided within the complex itself, with ophthalmology and physiotherapy services included. In addition, all the studios and workshops have a gym available with equipment for rehabilitation or exercise purposes.

The City of Porcelain is like a second home for the artists and artisans who work here. Thanks to the layout and facilities of the complex, social activities are frequent after working hours. On summer afternoons, games of domino are staged in the gardens forming part of the landscape of the City. On weekends, employees and family members enjoy the swimming pool and the park areas. And every day after work, the sports grounds are a rendezvous for tennis, basketball and fronton tennis players.

Life at the City of Porcelain transcends the employer-employee relationship. People work here, but they also study, play sports and make friends.

For staff members' children Lladró organizes many free time activities, such as camping trips, swimming and tennis classes, and language trips abroad. At Christmas time, Lladró always transmits joy to everyone, children included, by organizing a popular Parade of the Three Kings, during which presents and sweets are given out.

Once a year during what we call the 'socializing seminar', the City of Porcelain becomes a huge fairground, with employees coming with their families.

There are exhibitions and cultural activities, games, attractions and open-air paella competitions, and the walkways and gardens of this City dedicated to art are filled with the sound of music, laughter and fun. The children enjoy themselves the most, perhaps, and have the opportunity to see where their parents work. Some, in fact, become Lladró artists for the day.

So we can see that the people who work in the City of Porcelain share quite a lot more than their professional dedication to the field of art. They work together like a large-scale family, and they often spend their free time with their colleagues right on the premises, thanks to a broad range of facilities placed at their disposal for use on a daily basis. By contributing to the well-being of their associates and employees, Lladró ensures that life will be better for everyone involved in the field of dedication to porcelain art. Happy people in harmonious surroundings make better contributions to the creative process.

The years have passed, but the climate of companionship and cooperation created during the Lladró brothers' initial years has remained intact. One might say that in its essential character, the present-day City of Porcelain is the fruit of the development of their early workshop. Many years ago, the founders worked in close collaboration with their associates, sharing hopes and joys, time and efforts, in common. Today this spirit of closeness has been transferred to new

surroundings, but it is still highly palpable, attracting the attention of everyone who comes for a visit. The basis of all activities at the City of Porcelain is the same now as it was in its beginnings: the extraordinary artistic capacity of the Lladró family, their ability to make agreements and their intelligent criteria when it comes to selecting their team. These have been the reasons for their success in creating an atmosphere where creativity flourishes.

Social life at the City is therefore an important part of the overall picture. In a field in which the emphasis is on art, beauty, and the finer sentiments of life, it was entirely apropos for the founders to stress a well-rounded, harmonious atmosphere where people could be encouraged to bring out the best they have inside. The underlying idea was to ensure that art might spark up and burn brightly in the hearts and minds of men and women at the City of Porcelain.

The social events organized for Lladró employees include entertainment for children and adults (above) and demonstrations in which the kids get to see what their parents do at work (preceding page).

Some visitors who come to the City of Porcelain receive preferential treatment when it comes to visiting the studios and facilities, enjoying special, personalized attention. This is because they are members of the Lladró Society and have come to Valencia from many different parts of the world to see the place where their favourite figurines are brought to life.

The Lladró Society founded in 1985 is currently composed of more than 100,000 members around the world. These people are from different cultures and origins, but they all share the same concept of beauty and a passion for porcelain art.

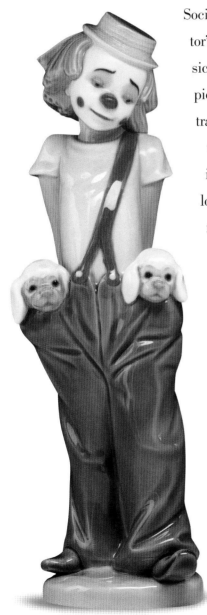

A Day in the Life of the City of Porcelain

THE SOCIETY OF ART LOVERS

Lladró creates various figurines each year intended specially for Lladró Society members. Because of their exclusive nature, they become collector's pieces. The Annual Lladró Society figurine is now an important classic, and has been ever since "Little Pals" first came out in 1985. These pieces, intended for private Lladró Society member collections, combine traditional Lladró quality with an incalculable symbolic and sentimental value. To satisfy demands from ambitious Lladró Society members looking for special porcelain pieces which are just as perfect as others but a lot more complex, the Society offers large-scale pieces exclusively for members. In 1992, the figurine "The Voyage of Columbus", a first-time-ever creation, was produced in the City of Porcelain with the aim of commemorating the Quincentenary of Columbus' Discovery of America. Since then, new limited series have been incorporated into the collection much to the delight of people who have been able to create a special site for them in their private collections at home.

The major milestones in the social life of the Lladró Society were the opening of the Lladró Center in New York in 1988, and the celebration of the 10th Anniversary of the Lladró Society in 1995, which brought together members and the Lladró family in a series of gala events held around the world. The sites were Santiago de Compostela, Toronto, Auckland, Madrid, Blenheim, Los Angeles, Chicago, New York, Modena and Valencia.

On the preceding page, "Little Pals", the first annual figurine. Left, the Lladró Society answers a need many people share: the love of finely-made porcelain pieces and the pleasure of collecting them. Below, "Guardian Angel", exclusive limited edition piece for members of the Lladró Society.

The gala events were highly memorable occasions for everyone who considers porcelain art to be a source of personal enjoyment and a common link shared with thousands of other people throughout the world.

3. UNIVERSAL ARTWORK

Like all cultural phenomena, the works of the Lladró brothers cannot be understood as isolated works of art. To understand them, we have to take into account the longstanding tradition of European porcelain art which they have adapted and developed in their own right. Lladró has renewed this tradition, perhaps better than many before them. They have given shape to an unmistakable style of their own which has not lost the virtues of the finest porcelain of the past while admirably expressing the feelings and sensitivity of people of our time. Thanks to this, Lladró figurines have become the finest emblems of artistic porcelain in the second half of the 20th century.

THE TRAINING STAGE

In these initial pieces the struggle to gain command of the difficult process of making porcelain can be seen. On this page, "Regional Dress", and on the following page, "Regional Dance", both modelled by Vicente Lladró and decorated by Juan Lladró in 1956.

The career of all great artists begins with a painstaking learning process characterized by continuous experiments in which one's debt to the past – to one's masters and forebears – is clearly evident. The Lladró brothers tackled this initial stage in conditions of particular hardship. Postwar Spain meant isolation and economic difficulties, and if mere subsistence was hard, it was even harder to find access to proper education and training. The fact that three young men from a humble farming family and educated in a impoverished country were able to lay the foundations for a company that was to rise to the forefront of international porcelain art is something that can only be attributed to an extraordinary will to overcome difficulties and an insatiable desire to learn and improve their lot.

The history of Lladró porcelain is the expression of this will, this constant search for perfection. The creations themselves speak louder than any other testimony of the trials and tribulations undergone by the three Lladró brothers throughout their lifetime. Their initial pieces show their struggle to master the difficult technique of making true porcelain. The creative spirit of Juan, José and Vicente pitched a prolonged battle with a material that was always wont to resist the dictates of man, especially if the conditions were not entirely appropriate. They combined wage-earning in a factory with continuous experiments in their parents' home, which took up much of their free time and also not a little of their earnings in a family that was not particularly well-off. It was only through sheer willpower and many years of struggle that Juan, José and Vicente overcame these difficulties and became master manufacturers

of porcelain. They gained a command of traditional techniques and were able to find new and imaginative ways to develop them.

Nevertheless, to ensure the viability of their global project, the Lladró brothers needed more than sensitivity, artistic skills, and long hours of work. They needed the support of other people. From the beginning they attracted excellent associates: artisans, technicians and sculptors. They inspired them with their own vision and drive and formed the foundations of what was soon to become the finest creative team in the world of porcelain art.

Over Lladró's 40-year history, this extraordinary group of professionals and artists has developed a repertoire which is extensive and varied, yet it shares common features that make it unmistakably Lladró. Despite the extensive palette of creations and the variety of participants in the complete creative process, there is an undeniable consistency of style in all Lladró works. This can only be explained by the special atmosphere existing within the walls of the City of Porcelain. The Lladró brothers supervise the daily tasks of the sculptors and approve each new model being developed, ensuring that every stage of production achieves the highest quality standards which have made them famous. For this reason, it can safely be said that Lladró porcelains are truly unique artworks with stylistic features of their own, having developed and evolved in a coherent manner.

After a few years, Juan, José and Vicente became experts in the manufacturing of porcelain figurines. In addition to commanding traditional techniques, they were able to discover new and imaginative technical solutions. On this page, "Ballerina Resting", and on the following page, "Ballerina with Rose", both made in 1957.

The works of the Lladró brothers have roots which are nourished by two complementary cultural heritages – Valencia's long tradition of arts and crafts, and the legacy left by significant creators of European porcelain over the last few centuries.

BEYOND TRADITION

Valencia has an age-old tradition in the art field, showing a special kind of Mediterranean flair. Over the centuries the region has always placed emphasis on its popular arts and crafts. All the ancient civilizations of the West contributed to the cultural fabric of this region. This can be seen in many details of daily life and in social customs. The festivities of the 'Fallas' are only one manifestation of the importance that art has in the daily life of the Valencian people. The attentive observer will be able to find many more noteworthy instances, such as the façades of buildings, the decoration of traditional homes and the innumerable examples of popular arts and crafts.

In the Lladró brothers' early works we can see the influence of two complementary cultural heritages: Valencia's long tradition of arts and crafts, and the legacy left by significant creators of European porcelain over the last few centuries. On this page, a portrait of Enrique Navas, painted by Juan Lladró in 1948. On the following page, "Lady with Cupid", a figurine from 1958.

The tradition of European porcelain from the 17th and 18th centuries also exercised an important influence on the Valencian region. For example, the porcelain factory in Alcora, Castellón province – an important production centre founded in 1727 – followed the style initiated by French porcelain, particularly that of Bérain, although there are other features that are more characteristic of Sèvres, Chantilly and Meissen. This reference to the Alcora porcelain production is especially significant because, in the words of the prestigious historian Vicente Aguilera Cerni, "Alcora is the closest precursor to Lladró today, due to their artistic perfection, their in-house work, their range of themes, their stylistic coherency and the stamp of prestige that the possession of their pieces represented."

Notwithstanding the diversity of styles and methods shown in works like these, close observation shows the outstanding artistic talents of the three brothers and their tendency to combine popular styles with the appeal of pure classicism. Above, an imperial vase decorated by Juan Lladró in 1953, and on the following page, "Old Salts", 1944, painted by José Lladró.

It is therefore no surprise that when Juan, José and Vicente Lladró began creating artistic porcelain, their first productions clearly showed the influence of references which were so close to them in spirit. Their initial works, like those of all artists in search of an expressive outlet, presented a variety of styles ranging from the traditional decorative ceramics of popular Valencian art to examples of academic works taken from classes at the Valencian School of Arts and Crafts. Some of these pieces, which form part of an early collection of works that was destined to become world famous, can be seen even today at the Lladró Museum in New York. Notwithstanding the diversity of styles and methods shown in these works, the observer is captivated by the outstanding artistic talents of the three brothers and their penchant for combining popular styles with other aspects that lean towards pure classicism.

"Acrobats", a ceramic piece decorated by Juan Lladró in 1944, is a good example of the influence of popular Valencian ceramics on the Lladros' first creations. Both its theme and its execution have an entirely spontaneous and vigorous look, which are the characteristic notes of traditional ceramics in this region.

At the same time José decorated a plate called "Old Salts". This work transports us to the pictorial universe of the painter Sorolla, due to its seaside theme and its use of light to show movement. The influence of this painter can be seen throughout the entire school of Valencian painting.

During Juan and José's years of art training, they delved into all genres of classical painting: still-lifes, landscapes, portraits, and anatomical sketches. This complete repertoire of motifs was essential for gaining command of the techniques required for producing a full range of decorative styles. Their initial creations already showed many themes that would characterize future Lladró collections: ("Advice to Sancho", "Don Quixote"), scenes with children and animals ("Tenderness", "Surprised Cat") or religious themes ("Jesus").

While two brothers strengthened their command of painting, Vicente made rapid progress in the field of sculpture, which he took up with the idea of complementing the talents of Juan and José. In his first works, made in the classical European style of porcelain production, Vicente demonstrated a talent for modelling and for creating ornamental compositions ("Urn").

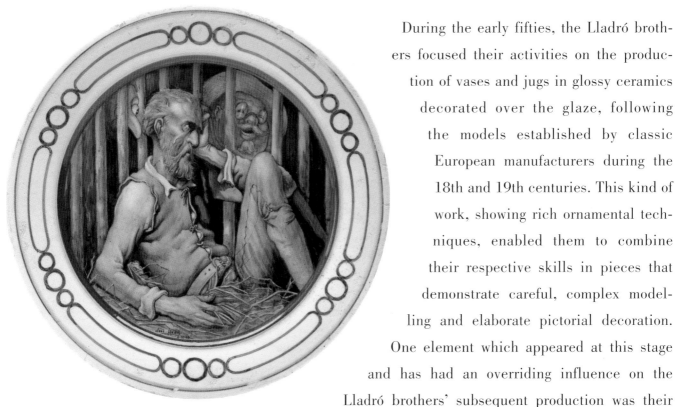

During the early fifties, the Lladró brothers focused their activities on the production of vases and jugs in glossy ceramics decorated over the glaze, following the models established by classic European manufacturers during the 18th and 19th centuries. This kind of work, showing rich ornamental techniques, enabled them to combine their respective skills in pieces that demonstrate careful, complex modelling and elaborate pictorial decoration. One element which appeared at this stage and has had an overriding influence on the Lladró brothers' subsequent production was their

These works show glimpses of the subject matter that would mark the future of Lladró works – characters from Cervantes, children and animals, and religious themes. On this page, above, "Don Quixote", painted by José Lladró in 1949; below, "Jesus", a work by Juan Lladró from the same year.
On the following page, above, "Tenderness" a creation by Juan dating from 1946; and below, "Surprised Cat" painted by José in 1943.

ability to model flowers. This was the start of their mastery in this field, making many of their creations from this period famous.

The year 1956 was a turning point in the career of the Lladró brothers who until this time had been focusing mainly on decorated plates and rococo-inspired vases. It was then that the brothers began making figurines in porcelain, reflecting the major tendencies of 17th-century European porcelain. Nevertheless, these initial figurines show glimpses of subject matter that would mark the future of Lladró works – country and courtly scenes, religious themes, regional folklore, animals and pets, and within this rich repertoire the field of dance shone with a light of its own.

"Ballet", dating from 1957, is one of the most representative figurines from this period. A rough analysis reveals a stylistic parentage of these works with figurines produced by the most famous ceramic manufacturers of the 18th century, such as Sèvres, Meissen and Capodimonte. The likeness is enhanced by the paleness of the ballerina's skin, a delicate hint of colour on her cheeks and knees, and the dark tones applied to her body and slippers. These effects were achieved using the traditional above-the-glaze painting technique, which is the application of pigment to the figurine after the porcelain has been fired, followed by another one or two firings of the finished piece.

A more detailed analysis shows the delicacy of her figure, which is simple, graceful and innocent, and much more elaborate than those of 18th-century porcelain. Of special note is the way the ballerina's tutu is made. Here, the Lladró brothers demonstrated their virtuosity in complicated porcelain lacework. They also undertook the challenge of presenting a figurine standing on one foot, deftly defying the laws of gravity. This is no mean achievement considering the difficulties of controlling a substance like porcelain, which is 'alive' and subject to unforeseeable changes during firing.

The creative period from which this figurine comes was brief, because soon afterwards the Lladró brothers found other solutions that would change the future of their work. Fortunately, however, this first fruitful time can still be seen in other beautiful pieces from the same period as "Ballet".

On this page, a vase decorated with a Romantic theme, a work by Juan Lladró painted in 1953. On the next page, "Ballet", a creation from 1957.

FROM CERAMICS TO PORCELAIN

At the end of the fifties, the Lladró style began to develop its most characteristic features. The most significant innovation to be developed at the Lladró workshops at that time was the substitution of ceramic materials with high-temperature porcelain. This important advance, without which it would have been impossible for Lladró art to develop, was only brought about by overcoming all the technical difficulties inherent in porcelain production. When this was achieved and the porcelain production process was sufficiently mastered, Lladró's sculptural abilities began to flower, with figurines acquiring more rhythm and movement. The artists were able to attain mastery of their materials and create works with no technical impediments. This newly acquired liberty resulted in creations that boasted skill and creativity, an intentional defiance of gravity, the creation of characters that became slimmer, svelter and more elongated, easily adopting the shapes and stances specified for them by Lladró sculptors. The perfection of firing techniques also enabled a qualitative leap to be made as far as decorating pieces was concerned. It was at this time that Lladró figurines acquired their characteristic look, being fired at high temperatures and painted under the glaze ("Lady from Valencia").

The sixties, which produced so many changes in ideas and art forms, also sparked off a renewal at the Lladró studios. The works of Juan, José and Vicente became bolder and more elongated, without abandoning the classical forms in which they were deeply rooted. Their pieces acquired longer, more elegant shapes during these years and Lladró sculptors created highly dynamic compositions ("Horse's Group").

Stylized forms marked the decade of the sixties, giving rise to characteristic works that had already begun to acquire international fame.

The popularity of Lladró porcelain in countries such as the United States and the United Kingdom provided proof of Lladró's universally appealing style and placed the Valencian firm, despite its modest dimensions, in a privileged position in the field of international porcelain art.

During these years, Lladró presented a number of pieces which are now considered to be authentic milestones in their career. Figurines such as "Sad Harlequin", a piece created in 1969, have become indisputable classics

The most significant innovation to be developed at the Lladró workshops in this period was the substitution of ceramic materials with high-temperature porcelain. On the preceding page, "Charm", a piece that still had on-glaze decorations, painted by Juan Lladró in 1958. On this page, "Lady from Valencia", from 1963, one of the first pieces made using current techniques.

in the Lladró lineup. It remained in the collection until the year 1993 – a quarter of a century – becoming an shining example of the timeless appeal of fine porcelain art. This palid, languid-looking harlequin, sitting next to his lute, is admired today just as much as he was on the very first day he was presented to porcelain art admirers around the world. Sadness reigns supreme in this creation, depicting melancholy and thoughtfulness. Throughout its life, it has moved people and inspired deep feelings in all those who have had the chance to see this expressive figurine.

Another masterpiece from this period is "Don Quixote". This recreation of the immortal hero brought to life by the pen of the great Spanish writer Cervantes, was created by Lladró in 1969 and has become one of the most successful figurines in the entire Lladró collection. For twenty-five years Lladró's Don Quixote has left the studios of the City of Porcelain en route to thousands of homes around the world. In fact, he has played a major role as a symbol of Spanish culture abroad.

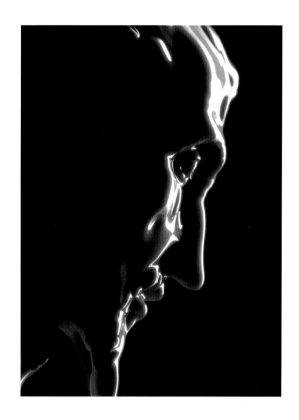

This recreation of Cervantes' immortal hero has become a symbol of Spanish culture for thousands of people around the world.

His elongated form transmits the spirit of the Man of La Mancha in a very special way, depicting the dreamer, the idealist, the gentleman whose contradictions were sometimes pathetic, sometimes profound, often comic. Only on the rarest occasions do form and content, style and subject, become so intimately bound up into one comprehensive whole as in this work, in which a character so often represented by artists of all kinds achieves one of his most significant incarnations.

The current appeal of these figurines demonstrates that the Lladró style of those years still keeps its hold on porcelain art admirers, beyond the whims of a certain age or period, magnificently expressing timeless, universal sentiments. The melancholy of "Sad Harlequin" and the spirituality of "Don Quixote" stand as imperishable values, depicted in fine porcelain, that well deserve the appreciation of future generations.

SAD HARLEQUIN

José Lladró

With "Sad Harlequin" we began a unique style which was different from anything which had been done in porcelain before. But at that time, no one could have guessed that in as little as thirty years people would christen it as one of the finest creations in our career.

I remember the time leading up to its creation as if it were yesterday. From the beginning we had always followed classical canons of beauty, with a tendency to represent well-rounded and proportioned forms, and the fact is that this brought us fame. The public appreciated our work. Nevertheless, this time the muses, who always seem to gather round when needed, inspired us to make something totally different.

We spent long hours working on this project, and we finally hit upon the elongated form of the harlequin. To attain this shape, we did lots of experiments with our model, because although we knew where we wanted to go, the way to achieve this was still hazy and imprecise. Our figurine had yet to take shape. And if possible, it had to be a very beautiful kind of shape.

The final result was simply dazzling because of its sensitivity, its appeal and the spirituality of this slender yet expressive figurine, which reminded us of paintings by El Greco or Picasso. Then we had to provide our figurine with the appropriate colouring, and fortunately, we hit the mark again – the light grey and brown tones we chose soon became an emblem of our later works.

"Sad Harlequin" was the prototype of a style that came into use in many other creations throughout the sixties. It was a style that became unmistakably connected to the name of Lladró. We had managed to place the hallmark of character on our creations, and people began to recognize them as ours in shop windows at home and abroad.

We were beside ourselves with joy, and this is a feeling that always returns to us when we see this figurine. And I can assure you that I do see it very often, normally at my own home, where for over twenty years it has stood guard by the portrait of me holding the "Sad Harlequin" that the artist Luis Arcas painted. He, like many others, knew how much of ourselves we gave in its creation, and the deep affection we hold in our hearts for it, so he resolved to leave me a personal testimony of this on canvas.

I love to contemplate it and reminisce on those years when we began renewing age-old techniques to create our own method of producing porcelain. Someone at that time said we had managed to give to the entire world what had hitherto been the privilege of princes and kings. That was a nice thing to say, and I feel very proud to think that we have given everyone, without exception, the chance to become princes and kings. And if just one of our figurines, perhaps our melancholy harlequin, manages to win only one heart, a whole life's work will have been worthwhile.

WATCHFUL GAZELLE

Vicente Lladró

It is a difficult task to single out one figurine when you love all the creations you make. To choose just one piece means to ignore everything else that we have made for the last forty years. This is a major challenge, because there is something very special in each and every one of our pieces.

If I stopped to reminisce about my preferences, they would be sure to include "Coiffure" or "Three Girls", or specially, "Holy Mary", because this was the figurine my brothers and I dedicated to the patron saint of Valencia. The public welcomed it with authentic devotion, making it an enormous success. I might also be tempted to choose our creations highlighting flowers, whose petals are fitted into place one by one, showing so much painstaking labour, such patient skill. The more work that goes into creating a piece, the more human feelings it contains, and this is something I always feel proud of.

But I trust you will allow me to go back even further in time and pick out a piece which I feel particularly strongly about. This figurine called "Watchful Gazelle" brings back many fond memories of bygone days.

In those days, the relationship we had with each of our creations was so intimate, so absolute. We were directly involved in each and every stage of creation. We modelled, decorated, and placed each piece in the kiln ourselves, impatiently waiting long hours for the final result, after the trial by fire. This was the test that would make or break all our work. Back then, anything could go wrong, upsetting the whole process. But these experiences provided us with the practical touch that we have passed on to our artists today.

"Watchful Gazelle" is not a spectacular piece, although I think you will agree that it combines simplicity, charm and delicacy. In the animal kingdom, the gazelle is the symbol of elegance, and throughout the history of art it has been an emblem of the human soul, of mankind's sensitivity. It also transmits tenderness and innocence, because of its association with our childhood memories of Bambi. All these factors join together in a figurine that has always charmed adults and children alike. It certainly has captivated me. I have very special feelings for this gazelle of ours, not only because of its unmistakable artistic qualities, but because it is one of the very first figurines exemplifying the wonders of porcelain manufacturing. The look in that gazelle's eye calls up memories of an enchanted age. And I suppose that for this reason I have reserved a special place for the "Watchful Gazelle" in my office, and in my heart, too.

PRAISED THE WORLD OVER

With the arrival of the nineteen seventies, the Lladró brothers reached their artistic maturity. The proportions of their figurines made a partial return to classical canons while presenting an extraordinary mastery of details. Although this led to greater realism, the kind of reality that was depicted always harmonized with that special vision of the world that Lladró reflects in all their works. Figurines made by Juan, José and Vicente showed a special feeling for the more positive and more pleasing aspects of reality. Goodness and beauty come to the fore in each figurine, whether in the sweet expression on a youth's face, or in the dynamic powerful form of a galloping horse.

Together with the Lladró brother's artistic maturity came international recognition and the fulfilment of a dream: the small artisan workshops had finally become the famed City of Porcelain, a complex where porcelain artworks were created for subsequent shipment to every corner of the globe. It was a time of unflagging efforts and non-stop activity. It was a period in which the Lladró brothers experienced unparalleled growth at the company without ever abandoning their principles of handcrafting, hand painting and achieving the maximum quality in all their creations. After all, these were the fundamental concepts which made them famous in the first place.

During these fruitful years, the Lladró brothers kept their creative abilities intact. Far from leading them into an attitude of complacency and comfort, the enormous success of their creations throughout the world served as a stimulus for them to embark on new artistic adventures. After meticulous technical investigation, they began to work with a new material in which they discovered a whole new world of expressive possibilities. When they began creating in Gres they found a much broader field for their abilities, thereby increasing the spectrum of styles that Lladró artists might use. The surface of Gres pieces could be given a new range of textures. Instead of smooth glossy looks, Gres provided new matte tones with a life of their own. Even the figurines themselves became more vigorous, more powerful, as Gres gave them new life. The special properties of Gres are particularly appropriate for the expression of themes that have always formed part of the Lladró universe, but could now be given a new lease on life. This is especially true of pieces representing animal life. Thanks to the powerful earthy tones and natural textures

From the 1960s, Gres gave Lladró artists a much broader field for their creative abilities. Here, "Passionate Dance", from 1973.

of Gres, birds such as eagles, grebes, owls and others look like they will almost take flight because of their remarkable vitality. Lladró artists found that Gres gave them the ideal medium for the development of their sculptural abilities, as shown in the strength and beauty of works like "Passionate Dance".

The classical purity of Lladró works acquires a new dimension thanks to the strength of Gres. Here, "Peace Offering", 1985. On the following pages, "Eagles Nest", 1981, and "Rescue", 1978.

Although the Lladró brothers first experimented with Gres and explored its possibilities in the sixties with the elaboration of vases, it was not until the seventies that the first Gres figurines actually appeared.

In 1970 the very first piece was brought out, showing a chimpanzee holding its baby. Next came a crouching cat, a pair of Gothic monarchs, a bullfighter, a Picasso-like mural and even some undecorated white pieces, very similar to the bisques of the 18th century. This was an offshoot of the first experiments in this material that the Lladró brothers made back in the fifties.

The year 1971 stands as yet another landmark in their career, because it marked the launch of a unique composition that stands out for its sheer size. The figurine was "Tahitiana", the largest piece ever created by Lladró until that time. It stood 112 centimetres tall (44½"), towering above the other creations, and presenting dramatic force and seductive charm. This creation offered warm textures and a harmonious combination of decorative glazes.

It was an exotic piece representing a native from the island of Tahiti, holding a jug on her head. Of note is the pictorial work done on the skirt worn by the young girl. Because of its meticulous detailing it looks much more like the traditional decoration done on porcelain vases.

Left, "Tahitiana". On the following page, "Mother Kissing Child", 1976.

SEEKING NEW CHALLENGES

Experimentation with new materials was only part of the picture as the Lladró brothers continued their search for new means of expression. The seventies was a time during which the City of Porcelain simply bubbled with new ideas, new projects, new trials and tests. Innovative subjects and themes were brought into play, in addition to new forms of expressing the same themes as before. Springing from the same interest in history and classical cultures that Juan, José and Vicente had always demonstrated, new creations appeared under the names of "Faun", forming part of a series inspired by mythology, and "Shakespeare" (page 142), which was a representation of the immortal playwright in the eyes of the Lladró brothers – an example of how history's giants became part of the Lladró repertoire.

In addition to the realistic pieces – which are by far the most frequent in Lladró's production – other works began to appear in which the emphasis was on the pleasure of producing purely decorative and ornamental works. This was the case of "Girl Offering Ceramics", where geometry plays a major role in the composition to create a purely decorative effect.

The quality achieved by the studios at the City of Porcelain in this period encouraged the Lladró brothers to undertake the challenge of creating more ambitious works. Thus the first limited series were conceived. These were more complex pieces where greater attention had to be paid to the technical details. They incorporated the added value of having limited editions, like other serialized works in the field of the fine arts. "Familiar Rallye" (page 143) is one of the first compositions made following this new concept. It was a

In addition to realistic pieces, which are the most frequent in Lladró's production, other works began to appear emphasizing the pleasure of purely ornamental works. On this page, "Girl Offering Ceramics", 1972. On the following page, "Faun", 1971.

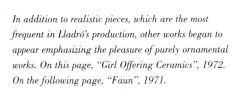

complex creation in which a number of characters combined to set a scene that was full of humour and dynamic movement. It demonstrated the skills of Lladró artists and their capacity to observe and portray the details of daily life. "Familiar Rallye" represented a new milestone in the development of Lladró and paved the way for the large-scale compositions that the three brothers would undertake in the future. This figurine had a series limit of 750 pieces and was one of the first limited series figurines in the history of Lladró.

Right, "Shakespeare", 1977.
Great historical characters become
part of the Lladró repertoire.
On the following page, "Familiar
Rallye", from 1971, one of the first
Limited Edition pieces made by Lladró.

An antique automobile including chauffeur and passengers creates the driving force for this figurine. Honking the horn, the intrepid chauffeur drives along out-of-the-way dirt roads. A little dog, responding to the chugging of the engine, leaps up to bite the driver, who deftly wards it off without losing control of his vehicle. The figurine portrays a turn-of-the-century scene with irony and skill. "Familiar Rallye" has become the delight of old-time fans and all porcelain aficionados with a sense of humour.

A few years later, the Lladró brothers took another step forward in their search for works that were increasingly ambitious and complex. This is how the Elite collection was born, composed exclusively of pieces of outstanding artistic and technical qualities, destined to form part of a select group of masterpieces in the Lladró repertoire.

One of the first pieces that entered the Elite collection was "Hunting", a dynamic composition of extraordinary realism in which the sculptor shows great skill in capturing the movement of the people and animals depicted in this hunting scene. Also belonging to the Elite collection is "Ducks at the Pond" (page 149), yet another example showing Lladró artists' refined realism and power of observation in representing detailed nature scenes.

Soon afterwards, Gres provided additional landmarks in the Elite collection. In "Playing Cards" (pages 146 and 147) the rich colours and multiple textures provided by this noble material breathe life into a dynamic scene which was inspired by characters from Spanish Golden Age literature.

Some representative examples of works
from the exclusive Elite collection.
On this page, "Pheasant Vase";
on the following pages "Hunting"
and "Playing Cards".

DUCKS AT THE POND

Juan Lladró

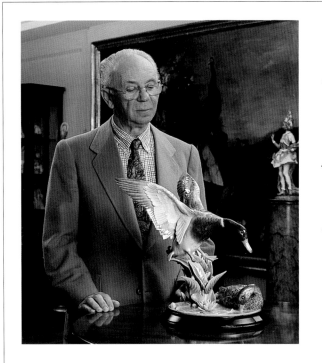

It's a beautiful morning, still a little chilly because it's so early. The sweet smell of orange blossom tells us we can look forward to a fine spring day. The birds sing, happy that dawn has come. Their chorus breaks the morning silence harmoniously, adding to the joy of a new day. The sun has just appeared over the horizon and spreads its warm rays over the land, chasing away the dew, lighting it up to reflect rainbow colours, looking like tiny diamonds in the crisp country air. I am surrounded by beauty, perhaps even more so than usual, because I have just awakened from a dream in which I saw my "Ducks at the Pond", my favourite piece. Now I am awake, but I fall into an early morning reverie,
because my dream from the night before reminds me of those rare days when an escape from my business affairs leaves me time for birdwatching on the shores of the lake next to my local golf course. Waterfowl take flight in the early morning, surveying the terrain perhaps, returning later with outstretched wings and landing with a splash on the water. They flap their wings, preen themselves, and then dive head-down into the water. They dive down and come up quacking, breaking the morning silence anew. Their beautiful plumage and graceful silhouettes have caught my eye on so many occasions. The way they waddle clumsily on foot contrasts sharply with their expert flying abilities. I watch them take flight once again, gaining speed and cruising effortlessly through the air, looking like aeroplanes slicing through the sky. Man compares them to his planes, but the duck came long before. And the ducks that Lladró captures in sculpture have been flying the skies for millions of years, never going out of style. Man's flying machines are made and then phased out within a few years. Lladró models, based on nature's creations, will still be fully up to date for many more years to come, as long as man does not clip their wings first.*

After this early morning daydream that recalled so many pleasant moments from the past, "Ducks at the Pond" brings me back to reality, as I contemplate their pure, graceful shapes so skilfully reproduced. As I enjoy looking at this piece that we made in a limited edition for a fortunate few, I come to the conclusion that "Ducks at the Pond" is surely one of the most outstanding pieces we have ever created, and I am certain our collectors, who appreciate the matchless beauty of fine porcelain, will want to enjoy more creations like this in the future.

In the eighties, the Lladró family continued their unceasing search for new forms of expression in their creations. This resulted in the birth of new collections that enhanced the scope of porcelain masterpieces that were already known and admired around the world. Pursuing a new concept in Lladró art, the Sculptures collection remained faithful to the spirit that guided all Lladró works, but took its inspiration from classical works of sculpture. These pieces were strictly confined to short run limited editions, and artists at the City of Porcelain placed all their abilities into the creation of works that come close to the finest works in the field of statuary art; with solid monochrome pieces that combined the delicacy and sensitivity of the Lladró style with the serene monumental size of the purest of classical sculptures. In works such as "Youth" and "Bather", the nude human body – one of the fundamental motifs of classical art – enabled Lladró sculptors to demonstrate their extraordinary command of modelling in clay and the capacity to create prototypes of timeless beauty.

In "Jesus of the Rock" (page 153) the human body in all its expressiveness, acquires a new dimension within the religious theme that has frequently been represented in Lladró creations. The body of Christ seems to emerge from the rock in which it has been sculpted, in a work of monumental force exemplifying the multifaceted creative capacity of the artists working in the City of Porcelain.

THE FUTURE OF PORCELAIN ART

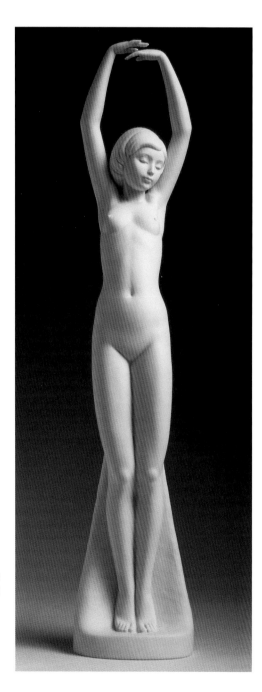

Pieces from the Sculptures collection combine the delicacy and sensitivity of the Lladró style with the serene, monumental size of the purest of classical sculptures.
Here, "Youth", and on the following page, "Bather", both from 1983.

With the significant title of Caprichos, meaning 'caprices' or 'whims', a new collection was initiated in 1987 with the emphasis on unique pieces in which the imagination of Lladró artists was unleashed and left to follow the fancy of the creative spirit. The pure pleasure of creation can be seen in the delicate lacework and flowers, which are two of the elements that have enhanced Lladró figurines ever since their early beginnings. In these pieces they acquire a prominent role, and are imbued with all their decorative power. The tranquil beauty of the young maiden represented in "Bust with White Veil" is highlighted by the fine porcelain lacework which is translucent and flowing, so skilfully moulded by Lladró artists.

On this page, "Bust with White Veil", 1988, from the Caprichos collection. On the following page, "Jesus of the Rock", 1989.

As one of the most innovative collections in the Lladró universe, Goyescas is only comprised of limited series pieces which preserve all the intense freshness and spontaneity of the artist's rough model serving as the starting point of other kinds of work. Each fold of a dress, each wrinkle on the skin, shows the skilled hands of the artist and how the forms have been built up one by one to create a singular composition. In "On Our Way Home" the porcelain seems to come to life all of a sudden, inspired by the flowing wind, creating an ensemble that depicts extraordinary dynamism and an expressive force that captivates the eye.

On this page, "On Our Way Home", 1988, a piece from the Goyescas collection. On the following pages, "Garden Party" 1988 and "XVIIIth Century Coach", 1985.

Aesthetic innovation, manifested in collections such as Goyescas or Caprichos, would never have been possible were it not for ongoing technical research into new materials and new processes. This is what enables Lladró artists to use the appropriate medium to express their ideas and to develop all the potential of their creativity, imagination and love of art.

In line with the new creative adventures undertaken by the Lladró brothers, their most characteristic and well-known productions in glossy porcelain continue to offer new and ever more ambitious ideas. Some of these also became veritable milestones in a collection of works which has now become a classic in 20th century decorative arts. "XVIIIth Century Coach" (pages 156 and 157) became the most complicated and expensive piece in the Lladró collection for a number of years. It is a sculptural composition

measuring 110 centimetres (44") in length, composed of four horses and five characters, a full range of accessories, and, above all, the kingly coach itself – an elegant berliner in the Baroque style inspired by original models housed in the Coach Museum of Lisbon. "XVIIIth Century Coach" gave way to diverse creations of a similar nature, the most notable of which was "Outing in Seville" (pages 164 and 165). This was a typical Andalusian carriage, re-created in faithful detail, which transports us in spirit to one of those famous May Feasts of Seville during which everyone has such a joyous time.

Despite the fact that it is much smaller in size than the pieces mentioned above, "Flowers of the Season" also awakened a great deal of admiration among the public. This was because it has such exuberant floral decorations. Since its creation in 1983, this piece has enjoyed great popularity among art lovers around the world who have unanimously recognized the value of the painstaking craftsmanship that went into it.

Below, a detail of "XVIIIth Century Coach", 1994. On the following pages, "Flowers of the Season", and "Cinderellas's Arrival".

Roses, tulips, daisies, carnations, gladioli and other varieties form a composition that totals over 310 different flowers, all made petal by petal by artisans with long years of experience at the City of Porcelain in Spain. In addition, twenty-seven different colours were used in decorating it, achieving a faithful reproduction of the true colours of all the flowers and plants, within the limits of the figurine's chromatic balance. This piece is so complex that it requires over fifteen days of meticulous work for it to be fully assembled.

"Flowers of the Season" belongs to that select group of figurines which admirers simply cannot resist. People feel they have to look at it again and again, being captivated by its array of

fanciful flowers and pretty petals that only need to give off their sweet fragrance to be thought real. Over the years, this piece has become one of the most popular Lladró creations. But Lladró creativity did not stop there.

Following these impressive pieces, the Lladró brothers pushed their limits even further, working on projects that have put all their creative capacities to the testing bench once again, challenging the capacity and ingenuity of their team of artists. Thus, in 1993, "Cinderella's Arrival" was born, a monumental composition with a profusion of accessories that required two years of intense work and the combined skills of forty-four artisans, artists and technicians.

In 1995, Lladró artists undertook a new journey once again by combining in one and the same piece all the subtle qualities of glossy porcelain with the rich textures and intense colours of glazes which had formerly been used only with Gres products. This is how they achieved an innovative combination which can be seen in the composition "La Menina", a creation that opens up new pathways for an extensive and highly fruitful artistic career. It is a career which has produced unmistakable universally known and internationally admired works of art. They are works which, on their own merits, have now become the single most important manifestation of porcelain art of the entire 20th century.

On the following page, "La Menina", 1995, a detail of which is shown on this page. On the following pages, "Outing in Seville".

4. SOURCES OF INSPIRATION

Despite their uniformity of style, Lladró works present a never-ending variety of themes and subject matters, like a precious stone with thousands of facets. Creators at the City of Porcelain are consummate artists, and as such, they are restless, inquisitive and open to new ideas that might enrich their work. Creativity feeds on life itself, and everyday emotions and experiences may often serve as the basis for a work of art, transmitting feelings and sentiments we all share. But life is a many-splendoured thing, and therefore, Lladró creations are rich, diverse and as surprising as life itself. Nature, daily life, literature, music, religion – all things good and wonderful, noble and pure, are the raw materials that form the basis of all Lladró artwork, thanks to the magic of fine porcelain.

SCENES FROM DAILY LIFE

Ever since the beginning of time, artists have looked to their immediate environment in search of inspiration for their creations. Primitive painters in caves and rock shelters carefully observed the animals they hunted and depicted themselves carrying out a variety of domestic chores. As he developed, man always found a place for images of daily life in addition to all of his gods, kings and heroes. In some periods, the 'minor' themes prevailed, even contributing to great moments in the history of art. Dutch painters in the 17th century, for example, produced numerous masterpieces in the form of simple still lifes, scenes of local customs and manners or interiors of well-to-do homes.

Yet despite the formal distinction between 'greater' and 'lesser' themes, day to day life has always appeared in one way or another throughout the different historical periods. In grandiose religious or mythological compositions from the past, we find that the main theme is accompanied by details that illustrate the way people from that age worked, played and lived out their particular lot.

European porcelain has also stood out, ever since the early 17th century, because of the attention it has always paid to scenes from everyday life, even when the authors of such works of art normally idealized their creations by converting the characters into refined members of the court or landed gentry in a bucolic world.

Lladró porcelain reflects this courtly tradition by producing works that strike a balance between the faithful

On this page,
"Away to School".
On the following page,
"Maternal Joy".

representation of reality and a more personal vision of the world that includes the imperishable values of goodness, tenderness and beauty. From this very special point of view, artists at the City of Porcelain have created a huge number of pieces which simultaneously integrate the unmistakable universe of Lladró with skilful recreations of the lives of men and women from the present.

Lladró artists are capable of finding inspiration in surprisingly diverse ambiences, from Oriental scenes to traditional fairy tales, showing human innocence and feelings. By depicting such moments in their charming creations, they demonstrate their skills in using children's games, parental love and scenes from the home as starting points for masterpieces in porcelain.

The history of Lladró is the history of a family. The support of their parents was vital to Juan, José and Vicente when they were just starting out on their own. Close collaboration among the three brothers, and later on among

Shown here, "Big Sister".
On the following page,
"Portrait of a Family".

their children, was a key factor in the success of the company. Family harmony formed part of the foundations of the company from its very beginning and contributed to the way the Lladrós perceived the world around them, as exemplified by a large number of creations.

The Lladró brothers represented their own parents in some of their early works, which were full of affection and tenderness. These are now on display at the Lladró Center in New York. In these early creations we can see the beginnings of what would become one of their major sources of inspiration in their future works.

We can therefore see scenes showing the intimacy of the home, the strong ties between father and son, mother and daughter. These have long been one of the favourite subjects of Lladró artists and also the most appealing for the public as well. This is not surprising. There are few values as

On this page,
"Fishing with Gramps".
On the following page,
"A Family of Love".

universally upheld as that of paternal love, because it is capable of inspiring people of all religions and all cultures.

Motherhood is also one of the fundamental themes in the history of western art. First it was holy in nature, in the form of majestic madonnas and tender mothers with babes. Later, non-religious works that were just as inspiring were created, paying homage to the intense, mysterious link between mother and child which has fascinated artists of all ages.

Mothers created by artists at the City of Porcelain renew this ancient tradition in pieces showing strength and fragility while at the same time presenting power and delicacy. This eternal theme highlighting maternal love takes on a new life thanks to the striking situations as well as the delicate graceful gestures devised by the artists.

Complementing the motherhood theme, we come to another major source of inspiration for Lladró artists, which is the world of children.

Childhood represents adventure, curiosity, discovery. It is the time when we see everything with innocent eyes, the period when we feel at one with nature and the world.

Children stand out in many of the creations from the Lladró studio. Childhood is an inexhaustible never-ending source of material. There are children of all nationalities, races and cultures, either playing, studying or daydreaming, often accompanied by their pets, which may be dogs, cats, or animals of a much stranger kind. In every scene, in every new game, in each mischievous look, we rediscover a remnant of our own childhood.

Shown here,
"Meal Time".
On the following page,
"True Affection",
a masterpiece by
Fulgencio García, with
metallic matte glaze.

We discover happy moments that were buried in our memories, now awakened after long years of slumber. Lladró artists manage to reignite these feelings in their creations, and when we look at them the memories all come back to us as if they were yesterday. At times like these we recover the happiest moments of our lives, our most cherished memories are now played out before us by our own children.

It is precisely in such little things in life, in those daily miracles, that we can find the deepest values, the finest feelings. These are feelings that provide us with fleeing moments of happiness that give renewed value to our lives.

On this page, "The Old Fishing Hole".
On the following page, "Cherish".

When we observe how nature gives life to each of her creatures, we can do little else but admire her and conclude, as Victor Hugo did, that the artist should have no other model than nature itself.

Sources of Inspiration
NATURE IS BUT ART

This, at least, is what countless generations of artists have also felt. Century after century they have used nature's resources, either realistically or imaginatively, as subject material, depicting the flora and fauna of landscapes near and far. From primitive art down to the present many different schools have enriched our interpretation of the world with their own particular visions of the world of nature around us. Time and again, western art has searched for models of true beauty in nature – from classical mythology to Christian iconography, to Medieval bestiaries, to Baroque fauna and flora, not to mention Flemish scenery and the soul-stirring Romantic movement of more recent times.

Lladró has also placed nature upon a pedestal and used her as a major source of inspiration. In numerous pieces, in either porcelain or gres, Lladró artists have recovered the beauty and the power of the animal world.

They are usually compositions that

On this page, "Flock of Birds".
On the following page, "Swans Take Flight".

awaken our feelings because they retain the purity, the nobility and the perfection of the animals they depict.

Each material used to create a Lladró animal figurine contributes its particular expressive force to the recreations made from the unending diversity of nature. The rich texture of gres figurines therefore manages to evoke all the vitality of the animal kingdom. The spectrum of tones provided by Lladró glazes and their earthy finishes highlight the characteristics of each species, bringing them to life before our eyes. At the same time, Lladró porcelain pieces transport us to the world of elegance, beauty and style, where serene hues and delicate forms evoke nature's penchant for perfection.

Horses have occupied a privileged place among the artistic manifestations of all historic periods. Ever since man first learnt to tame the equine family, they have become our inseparable companions, rendering faithful service to both princess and plebeians. In former times, they were of vital importance in times of peace and war, for personal transport and as beasts of burden. Even today, they still denote power and wealth. As always their noble looks and their strength have inspired admiration among animal lovers everywhere. For artists of all ages the horse has always been a supreme challenge, a call to give a faithful account of their elegance and dignity. Lladró has also paid homage to this creature in a number of memorable pieces. In these pieces, sculptors working in the City of Porcelain have taken great pains to model each form to show all the strength and energy of nature's creation, paying all due respect to this faithful companion of man.

Unlike horses, birds provide much more room for variation. Lladró's feathered friends come in

On this page,
"Thoroughbred Horse".
On the following page,
"Running Free".

almost as many shapes and sizes as real birds. Cranes, eagles, swans, ducks, owls, grebes, doves and herons all show their true colours in a collection that exemplifies attention to detail and respect for the true natures of these creatures, each of which is caught in a pose that looks so real. The proximity to Valencia of the inland lagoon of La Albufera has helped Lladró to become well versed in bird lore, as this area is one of the largest nesting zones along the Mediterranean coast. Artists have found it easy to seek models for their observant eyes and skilful hands. This rich coastal area – in which so many birds found it difficult to fit into the sky, according to the Spanish writer, Gaspar Aguilar – provides easy access for all kinds of species, whose rich plumage and swirling flights have inspired many Lladró creations down through the years.

Delicate flowers in porcelain are the emblem of the Lladró brothers' success in having incorporated all the exquisite beauty of flowers into their creations. To make such subtle and complex compositions, artists at the City of Porcelain need to have long years of experience and all the technical know-how acquired through meticulous work in the Lladró studios. Each flower petal is modelled separately and then mounted over the stamen so that no one flower is exactly the same as any other. Therefore the porcelain flowers made in this way for Lladró floral compositions show all the exuberance in shape and colour as real flowers created by nature. We might say, without exaggerating, that thanks to the skill and sensitivity of expert hands a series of bouquets are born that have practically everything real flowers have, except their fragrance.

Horses, elephants, crows and gazelles, eagles and herons, roses and peonies... each of these figurines inspired by the finest flora and fauna in the

world is a hymn to all the beauty that nature has placed within our reach. The entire ensemble of figurines featuring animals of all kinds is a rich artistic legacy that speaks of a profound respect for life and the need to preserve nature and the environment. These are timeless values that return with greater force than ever at the close of a millennium. Lladró artists, to be sure, have always remained faithful to nature over the decades.

"Gazelles". On the following page, "Grebes".

Sources of Inspiration
ROMANTIC VISIONS

Lladró artists are the creators of a complete universe. A universe composed of many different but equally marvellous worlds in which multiple facets of the real and the imaginary are peopled by delicate porcelain or warm gres figurines. But all of these worlds, despite their infinite diversity, show common features which unmistakably point to one and the same origin – none other than that special way of looking at the world shared by all Lladró artists. Each artist has his or her own way of tuning into this sensitivity, of looking at life and finding its meaning, of discovering goodness and beauty, the noble and valuable. Therefore, all Lladró creations offer the same realistic yet idealistic traits fused into one single whole.

"Little Harlequin".
On the following page,
"Spring Joy".

These distinguishing traits which define all Lladró creations are complemented by a unique way of executing themes, a special feeling when it comes to choosing motifs. These result in another feature of Lladró's extensive repertoire of works. It is what we call Romantic Idealization.

Melancholic clowns, ethereal maidens, proud riders on horseback, verdant gardens – they all form special spheres which are inseparable from the genuine Lladró style yet present a compendium of diverse influences derived from the fields of painting, literature and the theatre. They represent a tradition that transcends cultures and frontiers, enshrining Romanticism as a fundamental element of our culture. Archetypes from Italian comedy, refined gentlemen and delicate ladies from the Victorian age, young maidens dressed in idealized, timeless costumes, transport us to a far-away land, distant from the present, where no ugliness, pain or evil can ever reach us.

It is an imaginary country brought to life by artists who are fascinated by beauty and the desire to use rough clay to achieve a refined vision of a world overflowing with love, happiness and beauty.

Yet the Romantic mood goes beyond costume and dress. It is manifested in the theme itself, whatever it may be – from the simple yet fundamental expression of a young nude, to the way in which the sculptor softens the features of his figurines and arranges their anatomy to convey indolence or modesty. In Lladró nudes we witness the classical tradition, the yearning for eternal beauty which we can still see in the ancient Greek masterpieces where majestic expressions were given to the gods. But Lladró nudes are not necessarily goddesses, their beauty is neither cold nor distant, but rather the contrary – their creators have been adept at giving them an aura of

"Resting Nude".
On the following page,
"Youthful Beauty".

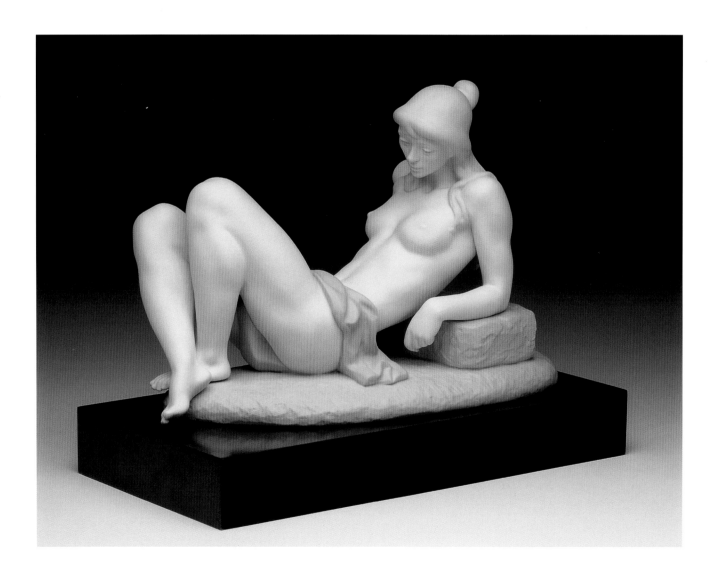

"Modesty". On the following page, "Far Away Thoughts".

sweetness that makes them even more idyllic, converting them into symbols of youth, of vigour and of grace.

Lladró creations are understood and admired by people on all five continents of the world despite cultural, religious and social differences. This is mainly due to the fact that many Lladró pieces inhabit an idealized world that corresponds to no particular time or place. It is a world we recognize as being near to us and thoroughly familiar because we can identify in it the authentic and genuine values which are common to all human beings. These pieces tell simple stories of love, tenderness and friendship, expressed by a

"At Peace".
On the following page, "Coiffure".

simple gesture, a smile or a melancholic expression. The love of a young girl for a horse, the old sailor recounting his adventures next to the sea – these are eternal images, universal symbols, evoking feelings that we can all share because they talk to us in a language that transcends frontiers, in a language that speaks directly to the heart.

Occasionally, some figurines contain more concrete references to a certain epoch or a certain place. These are scenes that tell us about the past, perhaps shrouded in the dream-like veil of mankind's collective memory.

A hunt on horseback, a conversation between a lady and a jockey, a ride in an antique automobile are themes that are full of the Romantic sentiment, taking a nostalgic look at times past, when the world was quieter, more refined, more human – a look that supercedes historical reality. Under the crystalline porcelain surface are the protagonists of stories that preserve all the flavour of customs, manners and lifestyles which seem to have been lost forever, but which can still be identified as an important part of our traditions and history.

On the preceding pages, "Fox Hunt".
Here, "Jockey and Lady".
On the following page,
"A Sunday Drive".

Not all, however, is nostalgia. Some of these pieces surprise us with their elegant yet ironic comments and their pithy sense of humour. "A Happy Encounter" is a romantic scene involving a gallant rider and an elegant young lady in an automobile, yet at the same time the rider's dog and the lady's pooch maintain a parallel eye-to-eye. There are other pieces that even achieve all the dynamics and mirth of a cinematographic gag, such as "Car in Trouble" in which an intrepid pair of early automobile enthusiasts lose control of their vehicle and provoke a stampede of terrorized geese.

Humour, tenderness, elegance and refinement are some of the ingredients that contribute to the attraction of these Romantic pieces which exemplify the talents and sensitivity of the artists who created them.

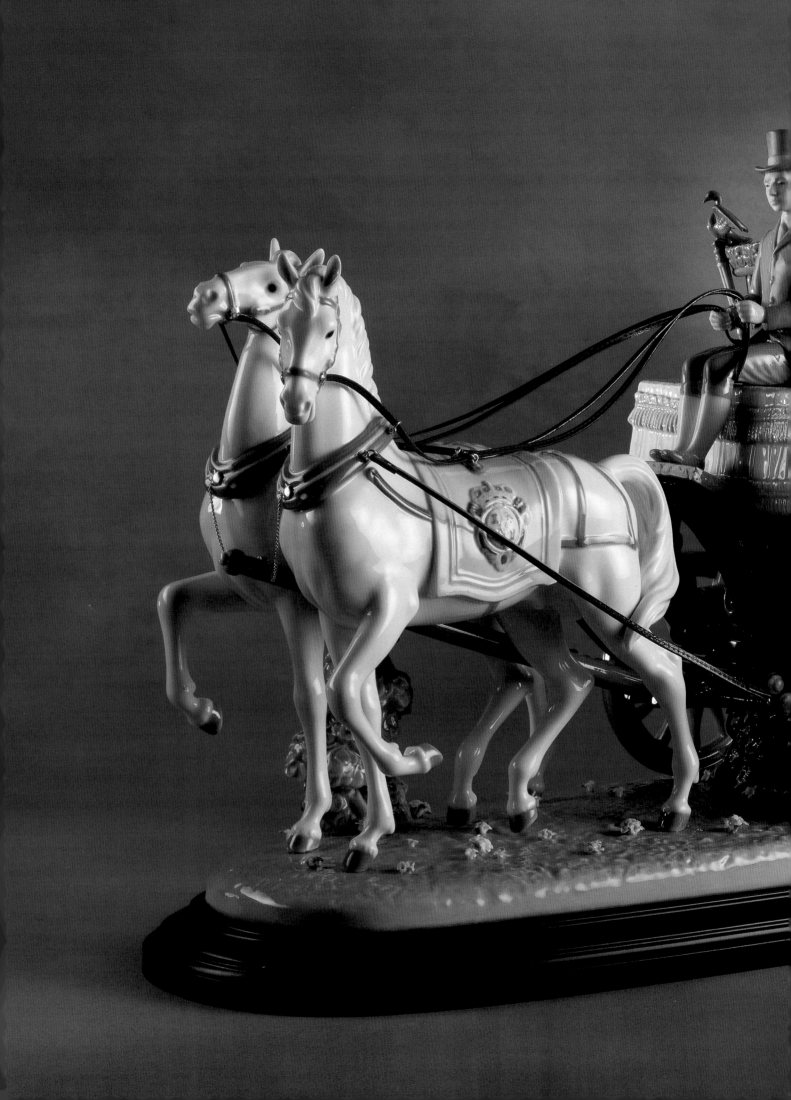

All true creators have two fundamental sources of inspiration: first, nature; and second, the masters of the past. Even the most original work of art is firmly seated on the solid foundations that culture has built up over the centuries, on a heritage which is common to all those who share the same background. This provides artists and non-artists with a sense of identity, the references that serve as guides to understanding ourselves and others and communicating what we have to say.

Sources of Inspiration
THE CULTURAL WORLD

Lladró drinks from this fountain. Artists at the City of Porcelain use music, literature, painting and dance as inspiration. Their models are subjects that transmit emotions in whatever kind of language they choose to use. Their themes are perennial and now belong to all of us through our cultural sensitivity.

This is why the artists from Spain who have created the best-known porcelain art in the world, cannot help feeling attracted by the figure of Don Quixote, undoubtedly one of the most universal creations this country has ever given the world. From the very first works personally made by Juan, José and Vicente, this Gentleman of the Sad Countenance has been portrayed in numerous creations. The Man of La Mancha is an immortal character, and has been used to depict a dizzying range of episodes described by Cervantes' pen. He has lent his elongated figure to Lladró with such a degree of success that some Quixote figurines have become the most emblematic artworks ever created at the City of Porcelain.

"Listen to D. Quixote".
On the following page,
"I Am D. Quixote".

Faithful to their cosmopolitan cultural roots, Lladró artists have always welcomed the influence of the great names of human culture, wherever they may come from. Thus, homage is paid to another literary genius, William Shakespeare, in the form of diverse pieces representing some of his most famous creations. "Hamlet" brings us an interpretation of the protagonist of one of the masterpieces of the English bard, wrapped in thought as he makes his famous monologue, now the universal symbol of human doubt and existential angst.

"Romeo and Juliet", just like the famed Prince of Denmark, transcend the written word to become porcelain reincarnations representing the paradigm of pure, eternal love – even for those who may not have read the work – capable of breaking down all barriers, even those of time, thereby continuing through the ages to successfully vanquish death.

On the preceding pages,
"Return to La Mancha".
Here, "Hamlet".
On the following page,
"St. Theresa".

Together with these famous characters from the field of literature bequeathed to us by the great minds of the past, other great names, real people but no less legendary, are provided from the history of mankind. These are the great historical characters, the men and women whose extraordinary achievements have left an indelible mark throughout time.

Napoleon Bonaparte, the general who became emperor of France and extended the heritage of the Revolution throughout Europe, was an exceptional statesman. He possessed a charisma that made him one of the first epic heroes of the modern world. In "Napoleon Planning Battle", we see him on his throne, crowned with an imperial eagle, studying his tactics before one of the numerous battles in which his army would face the next opponent, whether in the arid deserts of Egypt or the frozen steppes of Russia.

Whereas Napoleon created an empire through sheer manpower and force of arms, Christopher Columbus opened the gates to a new continent, allowing the European powers to reach outward in the 15th century. His determination and valour achieved something completely new – the bringing together of two worlds which had been separated by an unknown ocean until a handful of Spanish sailors under the leadership of the famed Genoan dared to cross it. "The New World" reflects the culminating moment of this adventure, when the admiral first set foot on the New World after his heroic Atlantic crossing, and took possession of those lands in the name of the Spanish King and Queen.

On the preceding page,
"Southern Tea".
Here, "Napoleon, Planning Battle".
On the following page,
"The New World".

Of all the arts, music is the one that most easily transcends the frontiers of time, distance and cultural differences. Without the usual limitations of language, the great classical composers were able to create an eternal discourse for the ear which appeals directly to the senses. Very few artists have been able to create works that have stayed with us for so long and in so many ways as the masters from the past like Bach, Mozart and Beethoven.

"Johann Sebastian Bach", the giant of the baroque age, created a monumental legacy that seems to gain in stature as the years and the centuries pass.

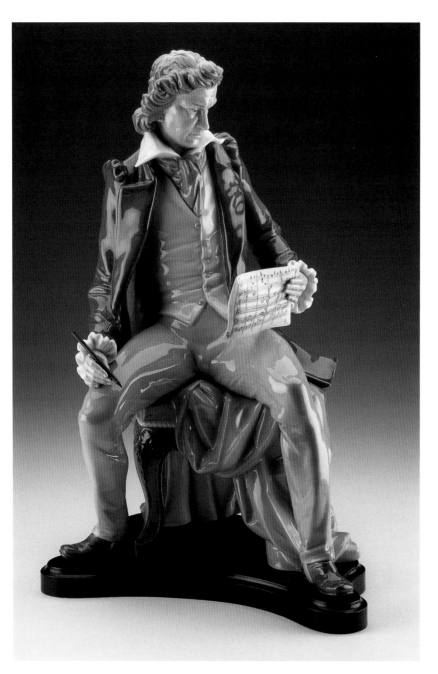

This famous composer is shown by Lladró artists in a special homage to the young Bach. This was the instrument, so fundamental to the religious music of the 18th century, for which Bach composed so many works that still have the capacity to enthrall the listener.

In the history of music Beethoven represents the birth of romanticism and its highpoint. His compositions, serene or passionate but always sublime, are counted among the best known and loved examples of classical music. The portrayal of this genius created by Lladró shows all the effusive, tormented character of a man who was capable of imagining some of the most beautiful sounds ever offered to the human ear.

Closely connected with music is the world of dance, an art in which the beauty of the human body becomes the primary means

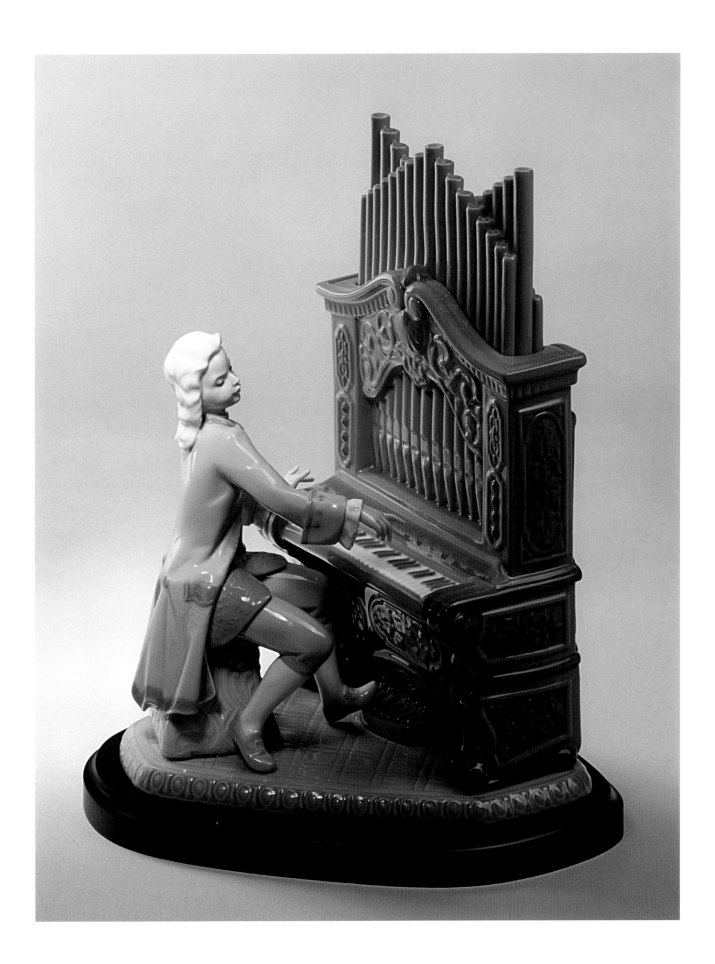

of expression. This field has also been a source of inspiration for the Lladró brothers.

Ever since their very early years, ballet figurines have played an important role in the Lladró collection. The first elegant ballerinas in any number of poses began to appear in the fifties. These were among the initial successes achieved by the Lladró team of artists. The ethereal lacework of their tutus or the precise equilibrium of their pirouettes on one single tiptoe gave the Lladrós ample ground for showing their talents and skills as sculptors and creators of porcelain art.

Since then, dance has long been a recurring theme, perhaps, one of the most characteristic of the entire repertoire at the City of Porcelain. It is a theme that Lladró sculptors, just like all other artists interested in showing the beauty of the human body, see as a fascinating challenge for their abilities, a unique occasion to replicate the complete range of expressions and movements that only a dancer's well-trained body is capable of producing.

"Before the Dance", "Closing Scene" and "Graceful Moment" are some of the pieces combining motifs borrowed from classical dance and the romantic, idealized atmosphere so characteristic of Lladró. These result in compositions which are full of dynamic elegance and grace, where porcelain seems to come to life and transform itself into skin, silk and tulle.

On the preceding pages, "Before the Dance". Below, "Closing Scene". On the following page, "Graceful Moment".

The history of Western art, from the Middle Ages until today, is closely linked to religion and the sentiments this evokes. For centuries the church was one of

the main propitiators of the arts, insofar as the majority of famous names from the past – from Michelangelo to Rodin, from Velázquez to Matisse – have provided us with major works of religious art. Some of these painters, such as Giotto, Zurburán or El Greco, were so totally identified with religion that it inspired the lion's share of their artistic work.

Lladró sculptors, as heirs and continuators of this tradition, have created many pieces in which the religious theme plays a major role, having borne important fruits in the field of Spanish art. Thus, in Lladro's "Blessed Lady", we find the spirit of Murillo – the baroque painter who created so many angelical Madonnas. "Saint Michael" and "Sorrowful Mother" are figurines rooted in iconography – a field in which Salzillo was pre-eminent. "The Burial of Christ" evokes spirituality and the expressive force of El Greco's works.

On the preceding pages, "Jesus in the Tiberiades".
Here, "Blessed Lady".
On the following pages, "Saint Michael",
"Sorrowful Mother" and "The Burial of Christ".

Elves, fairy godmothers as well as other fabulous characters and beasts all live in Fantasyland, a faraway land set in the imaginative fancy of man's mind, where Lladró artists are often wont to travel for inspiration, returning with a new addition to their fanciful figurine lineup. Mysterious unicorns, beautiful princesses and dashing princes inhabit this whimsical region where children feel at home – a place that Lladró porcelains help keep alive for adults.

TALES, MYTHS AND LEGENDS

Fantasy is intimately linked to poetry and beauty. The poet John Keats said of this relationship that "the sweet converse of an innocent mind whose words are images of thoughts refined is my soul's pleasure."

Children's fairy tales are based on characters and stories which have been nourished by the imagination of man for many long centuries. Stories that appear at first glance to be simple pastimes for innocent children are actually part of a millennia-long tradition receding back into the collective memory of all mankind. Oral legends and myths, and then the written word, have all served to enrich this legacy down to our time.

"Heavenly Swing".
On the following page,
"The Goddess & the Unicorn".

In the majority of popular traditions around the world, we usually find a mention or two of curious, diminutive beings called gnomes who possess extraordinary faculties. They are tiny forest dwellers who have a special penchant for interfering in the lives of men by making use of their magical powers. Sometimes kindly, sometimes mischievous, these funny little men with pointed caps are sure to continue with their pranks for a long time to come: for as many years, indeed, as the mind of man is able to imagine.

Contrasting with gnomes – which are masculine, forest-dwelling characters – fairies are feminine, aerial spirits.

These winged women figures inhabit the Land of the Fairies, a purely magical sphere, and are a much cherished tradition in the West. Since time immemorial man has maintained an ambivalent relationship with the Land of the Fairies, because some people seem to have been lucky enough to profit from their contacts with them, yet others have only paid testimony to their wrath. From simple bad luck to all types of spells and transformations, we often do not know what to expect from these mysterious little creatures.

Of all the mythical animals conjured up by the imagination of man, none is as mysterious as the unicorn. This shining white son of the equine family, a symbol of purity, is said to be able to cure a wounded or sick man with one touch of his magic horn. Legends tell us that only an innocent maiden can capture a unicorn. But when captured, this strange creature will inevitably die in a short time, unable to withstand captivity of any kind.

These and other marvellous creatures form part of mankind's legacy, and will continue to do so as long as we do not lose our ability to marvel at the unknown. Meanwhile, men and women such as the artists at Lladró are capable of converting such concepts into works of art that give wings to our fantasies.

On the preceding pages, "Leprechaun" and "Sprite". Below, "The Princess & the Unicorn". On the following page, "Love Story".

"Fantasia". On the following page, "Pegasus".

Whereas the infinite variety of nature's creations feed the imagination of the artists working in the City of Porcelain, the case is similar when it comes to different cultures spread over the five continents. Thus, from the inhospitable Arctic to the arid deserts of Arabia, from the American prairie to the shores of the Sea of Japan, Lladró artists find an unending source of inspiration for their works, nourished by exotic, colourful clothes, graceful dance rituals and mysterious ancestral traditions. These works form a compendium of the most significant and different cultural manifestations and are a homage to man's diversity.

Eskimos living in the frozen lands of the Polar Circle have inspired many figurines, especially in the Gres collection. This is because the warm, lifelike tones of the glazes used in Gres creations seem to alleviate the intense cold, whereas the subtle textures of Gres recreate with absolute faithfulness the feel of fur coats and collars used by the Eskimos in the garments that protect them from freezing winds from the North Pole.

Sources of Inspiration

ART KNOWS NO FRONTIER

"Arctic Allies".
On the following page,
"Desert People".

Much further south, we find "Desert People", showing two bearded travellers in the suffocating heat of the desert. This powerful Lladró composition shows two riders on their indefatigable dromedaries in a full array of detail, one standing and the other sitting on the sand. It is a homage to those who face the challenge of survival in the arid sea of sand. Once again, Lladró artists use Gres, with all its fine qualities, to create a scene in which we can almost see the blistering desert wind moving the headdresses of these noble people.

On their personal tour of the world's cultures, Lladró artists cannot help stopping off again and again on their own home turf, the land they love the most, simply

because they were born here. Valencia, the birthplace of Juan, José and Vicente, where their porcelain artworks are brought to life, the works that have given them a famous name throughout the world, has always been present in their creations, either explicitly on many occasions, or simply implicitly. The costumes of countrymen from the Valencian market gardens, the 'huerta', their customs, their festivals and folklore, have inspired numerous figurines which have become international ambassadors of the region's culture.

"Valencian Festival" and "Floral Offering" are two creations linked by a common element which is highly characteristic of both Lladró works and traditional emblems of the land of Valencia – flowers.

Valencia's patron saint, Our Lady of the Forsaken, receives a flower offering every spring during the Fallas festivities, which is a highly popular occasion. This offering is convincingly represented in these pieces and others that show a huge variety of flowers in all their splendour, with the rich colours and captivating textures that only Lladró artists have been able to produce.

The paella is the queen of Valencian gastronomy, a jewel in Spain's cuisine, an indisputably Valencian dish. However, as depicted in "The Paella", it is also the symbol of an entire lifestyle. It represents a way of life which is reflected in this composition where a family of farmers cook their midday meal over an open fire, using products from the local gardens, surrounded by their tools and trappings, bathed in the aromas of orange blossom, rosemary and thyme.

In "Mother" we find another vision of the rural world. The austerity of the lands of the interior, on the meseta of central Spain, is expressed here in a restrained yet powerful composition in which gestures are kept to a minimum, contrasting sharply with the vitality and vivacity of the Valencian landscapes. Nevertheless, the tenderness of a mother, her sweet expression and the sensitivity shown by every detail, are fully incorporated in the ensemble.

From the familiar and close-at-hand to the exotic and distant, the world offers a unimaginable range of possibilities that Lladró artists are constantly striving to embrace as they are avid for new motifs that might attract their attention and stimulate their creative abilities.

The Japanese live in a society in which ancient traditions and modern technology coexist, and they have learned how to apply their age-old philosophy to present circumstances. This means that the wisdom of their ancestors is still used to find solutions to the challenges of our complex world today.

This mixture of spirituality and pragmatism is only one of the characteristics of this country full of contrasts that surprises and inspires the western observer. Present-day Japan – so similar to the west yet so different – and the rich tradition of one of the most ancient and complex cultures in the world provide a major source of inspiration for anyone curious to learn more about the world.

Lladró artists have repeatedly shown their fascination with Oriental culture in general and particularly with Japanese society.

"Mother".
On the following pages,
"Oriental Music" and
"Oriental Garden".

The image of the traditional Japanese woman has been used in many Lladró figurines. With delicately decorated clothes, gentle demeanours and elongated forms, these pieces form part of the most attractive creations ever produced at the City of Porcelain. In many of these creations the elegant figure of a Japanese lady is accompanied by other traditional features of Japanese culture. For curious visitors embarking on a journey through the marvellous world of porcelain these are especially fascinating for us: bridges and other elements of Oriental architecture, majestic boats, exquisite flower arrangements, and so on.

And then come the contrasts again. The dazzling baroqueness of India brings us all its luxury and charm in "On the Road to Mandalay", a piece that immediately enraptures the senses, like the penetrating aromas of musk, curry, ginger and cinnamon in a colourful, raucous Middle Eastern market. The majestic elephant is decorated with a scene that might very well have come straight out of 'A Thousand and One Nights'. The proverbial Asiatic luxury is translated here into sumptuous decoration, painstakingly executed by Lladró ornamentalists, who pay all due respect to the exquisite and sophisticated aura of the Oriental court.

Thanks to "Hawaiian Ceremony" we make another long and extraordinary journey. The South Seas, the mythical destination of so

"Farewell of the Samurai".
On the following pages,
"On the Road to Mandalay" and
"Hawaiian Ceremony".

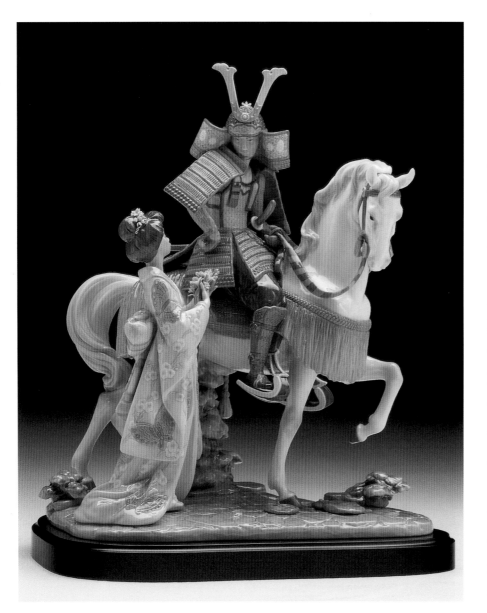

many adventurers in search of a lost paradise, welcome us with a spectacular demonstration of their ancestral rites. This piece reflects the sweetness and beauty of people from the Pacific in a harmonious composition that floats before our eyes as if it were gently being rocked by the tranquil waters of a Polynesian atoll.

This marvellous world of porcelain journeys can be visited in both space and in time. "Blue God" transports us to a lost civilization, which still astonishes us even today when we see its ruins half hidden by the equatorial jungle. The Aztecs created a refined yet brutal culture, perhaps one of the strangest that has ever coexisted with the west. Lladró artists allowed their imagination to fly off to this faraway land to recreate it in the form of a beautiful priestess caught unawares in an ancient unknown ceremony.

To finish this brief and necessarily incomplete sampling of Lladró's numerous creations offering a view of other cultures on all five continents, we return to Asia to meet "Philippine Girls". Here, ornamental richness, vivid colouring and the elegant movements of the Oriental dancers are the highlights, whereas in "Kitakami Cruise", taking inspiration once again from the Land of the Rising Sun, this Elite collection composition shows full attention to detail, ranking alongside other ambitious, difficult and highly decorative Lladró creations in porcelain art.

Above, "Blue God".
On the following pages,
"Philippine Girls" and
"Kitakami Cruise".

5. LLADRÓ IN WORLD MUSEUMS

True porcelain fired at high temperatures is a luxury today, a privilege from olden times, a complex substance that incorporates the added value of human intervention during production, handcrafted care in a world which is increasingly mechanized, automatized, uncontrollably replicated and serialized. Lladró, today, is one of the last great European porcelain factories still in operation, and without a doubt, is the most important artistic porcelain creator in the world in view of its production levels, its quality standards and its artistic achievements. In its own merits, Lladró is an heir to a centuries-old tradition in the field of artistic porcelain and the decorative arts, which were destined in former times to occupy prominent places in the homes of the aristocracy.

However, after perfecting the complicated porcelain manufacturing technique and pushing quality and artistic appeal up to the highest possible levels, Lladró has been able to place this material within reach of the public at large and has made it possible for many people around the world to enjoy the imperishable beauty of authentic porcelain – an art form reserved for the few until now. The significance of Lladró, therefore, is much more a question of an artistic achievement than a purely commercial endeavour, as recognized by cultural bodies of such importance as the Hermitage in St. Petersburg, the International Ceramics Museum of Faenza, the González Martí National Ceramics Museum of Valencia and the Fiftieth Anniversary Museum of Brussels, among others, which have incorporated Lladró works into their permanent collections.

St. Petersburg was described by Pushkin as Russia's "window on Europe". This impressive city was founded in 1703 by Peter the Great, and its monuments were designed by leading architects of the day brought in from all over Russia and Europe. The Baroque style came to full expression here and the beauty of the city has served as inspiration for many generations of artists and poets. Clear examples of its magnificence are St. Isaac's Cathedral, the Kazan Cathedral, and the former principal residence of the tsars – the Winter Palace – a Baroque masterpiece which now houses one of the finest museums in the world: the Hermitage.

Journeying through its halls, the visitor is taken on a tour of history. There are over two million works of art in the museum, including works by Leonardo Da Vinci, Raphael, El Greco, Ribera, Velázquez, Goya, Rubens, Rembrandt, Matisse, Picasso... And as of several years ago, Lladró has been added to the long list of illustrious names represented in the museum.

The mayor of St. Petersburg, Anatoly Sobchack, was deeply impressed after visiting the City of Porcelain, which formed part of a trip he made to Valencia, Spain, in 1991. During his visit he urged the Lladró brothers to stage an exposition of their work in St. Petersburg.

This exposition, held in the beautiful St. George salon, also known as the throne room, contained 121 pieces of the finest Lladró porcelain ever made.

THE HERMITAGE OF ST. PETERSBURG

"Don Quixote", a Lladró emblem and standard bearer of Spanish culture, forms part of the collection at the Hermitage.

During the opening ceremony, Mr. Suslov, curator of the Hermitage, spoke of the exposition's importance to the museum and to the people of St. Petersburg: "This display has taught us a lot about the tradition of porcelain art in Europe. Despite the fact that the Hermitage holds a collection of Spanish ceramics from the 17th century and a selection of 18th-century paintings, we unfortunately knew very little about modern art in Spain. For this reason we are thankful to Lladró for agreeing to exhibit their porcelain in St. Petersburg."

Since then, "Don Quixote", a symbol of Spanish culture, and "XVIIIth Century Coach" one of the most famous pieces by Lladró, form part of the exhibits in the permanent collection of the Hermitage of St. Petersburg, one of the world's major sanctuaries for timeless treasures in art.

Preceding page, Anatoly Sobchack, mayor of St. Petersburg, and Juan Lladró during the inauguration of the Lladró exposition at the Hermitage.
The other photographs show various details of this important exhibition held in 1991. Below, left, "XVIIIth Century Coach", one of the finest Lladró creations
forms part of the permanent collection at the Hermitage.

The Palace of the Marquis of Dos Aguas is an ornate 15th-century building counted among Valencia's finest monuments and housing the legacy of the Valencian scholar Manuel González Martí: porcelain, ceramics and other examples of the decorative arts. Pieces from Paterna, masterworks from Manises, relics from the Iberian past, examples of Greek treasures, a series of vases and lamps belonging to the Romans who once inhabited these lands, are some of the exhibits this illustrious Valencian researcher was able to collect for the museum, now know as the National Museum of Ceramics and Sumptuary Arts.

THE GONZÁLEZ MARTÍ OF VALENCIA

"Mancha Nobleman", one of the Lladró figurines in the González Martí National Ceramics Museum. On the following page, the extraordinary Baroque façade of the Palace of the Marquis of Dos Aguas housing the museum.

González Martí, founder and curator of the museum until his death, carried out an exceptional amount of research and classification of the treasures he was able to acquire, going so far as to collect carriages, clothing and ancient books. He was also responsible for sensitizing both individuals and institutions to the need to preserve the region's heritage. Without the help of these people he would have been unable to amass the important collection occupying the halls of this museum today. It is a collection which has grown with the times, incorporating major works by contemporary artists–works by Picasso and Benlliure are part of the museum holdings–as well as 16 outstanding pieces from the Lladró collection which are on display on the second floor of this palace museum.

A stroll through the richly adorned halls of the permanent exhibition provides a splendidly represented panorama of Valencian tiling from the 18th and 19th centuries. Other large collections include ceramics with metallic reflections from the 16th to the 18th centuries. These are mainly Catalan specimens from Reus and Valencian ceramics from Manises. Special mention should also be made of the pieces on display from the Royal Factory of Alcora, Castellón, showing four exceptionally well-construed mythological pieces representing the four elements.

The palace is a Gothic construction from the 15th century, yet it has been expanded and restructured many

times during its history. The painter Hipólito Rovira and the sculptor Ignacio Vergara were responsible for the splendid Baroque doorway added in the 18th century which shows an allegorical representation of the two Valencian rivers, the Turia and the Júcar, which cross the erstwhile estate of the Marquis of Dos Aguas. Dos Aguas means 'two waters', and refers to a township in the hinterland of Valencia province. This allegory is topped by a niche containing the image of Our Lady of the Rosary.

Above, a view of the patio of this ornate Valencian palace now converted into a museum. Below, "For a Ride", another Lladró piece exhibited in this museum.

In 1853, the new heir to the title undertook another transformation of the palace, which was basically ornamental in approach, converting it into

a truly eclectic building with the addition of Rococo and Neo-Empire styles and Chinese motifs. The façade was decorated with jambs and lintels and the balconies were fitted with balustrades. A few Gothic windows disappeared from the inner patio, being substituted by balconies with allegorical figurines in relief. Some halls were given trompe d'oeil effects and ceiling medallions and period furniture was brought into the Porcelain Room of the time.

Three decades after the first meeting between the Lladró brothers and the founder of the museum the same spirit of co-operation, encouraging them to work for a common cause, is still very much alive. This is demonstrated by the fact that Lladró has signed an agreement with the Spanish Ministry of Culture under which the company undertakes to finance the restoration of the Ballroom of the Palace. Through this initiative, the Lladró brothers wish to contribute to the recovery of one of the most emblematic institutions in Valencia with which they have always felt closely connected.

Below, one of the rooms in the Palace of the Marquis of Dos Aguas housing porcelain objects.

On May 21, 1987, Juan Lladró and his wife, Dolores Sala presented the piece "Pursued Deers" to Anne Marie Goebbels, director of the Bellevue Museum and to Henri de Meulenaere, curator of the Royaux Musées of Art and History.

Lladró in World Museums

THE FIFTIETH ANNIVERSARY MUSEUM OF BRUSSELS

As of that moment, one of the most emblematic pieces in the Lladró Elite collection became part of the impressive artistic patrimony of this Belgian museum. The donation ceremony reflected the outstanding recognition given to Lladró creations as fine examples of contemporary art in porcelain, and their incorporation into a prestigious institution whose holdings include some of the most important collections in the history of the decorative arts.

The Bellevue Museum forms part of Belgium's Royaux Musées, or Royal Museums, dedicated to art and history, which also includes the Hallepoort, the Japanese Pagoda, the Chinese Pavilion, the Museum of Musical Instruments and the Fiftieth Anniversary Museum. Recently, "Pursued Deers" was transferred to this museum, where it has been on display since the end of 1996 in the Repertoire Salon.

The Fiftieth Anniversary Museum houses numerous exhibits depicting the history of mankind from prehistoric times to the present, with examples brought in from diverse civilizations on all five continents.

The work of this museum goes beyond preserving and exhibiting its holdings. It plays a role as an authentic scientific institution dedicated to the study of history and art. To give the public a suitable picture of the rich heritage it contains, which is widely acclaimed in the scientific field, the museum is involved in important tasks of publicizing its scientific and cultural findings, careful-

Juan Lladró and his wife Dolores Sala next to Henri de Meulenaere, curator of the Royaux Musées of Art and History, and Anne Marie Goebbels, director of the Bellevue Museum, who were presented with "Pursued Deers".

ly exhibiting its permanent holdings and carrying out a special policy of staging frequent temporary exhibits. This is how the Fiftieth Anniversary Museum gives its visitors fascinating tours of the world of archeology and the history of art.

The museum was officially instituted by royal decree in 1835, soon after Belgium obtained independence from Dutch rule, with the founding of the Museum of Ancient Arms, Armour, Art Objects and Numismatics. But the heart of the present-day collection was gathered together many years before this. Some of the most outstanding exhibits had been well preserved in the Royal Arsenal and among these were the diplomatic gifts of the Dukes of Burgundy and the Hapsburgs, as well as curiosities and mementos including the cradle of the Emperor Charles, the blanket of Montezuma and the hobby horse of the Infanta Isabel.

After it was founded in 1835, the museum was housed in the Hallepoort, but it soon became obvious that more space was required. The construction of two pavilions in the Park of the Fiftieth Anniversary made it possible for some of the collections to be transferred. The museum was therefore integrated into a new project being undertaken by Leopold II which consisted of turning the park into a complex combining recreational facilities and a cultural centre.

Over the years, the museum's collections have been enlarged thanks to important private contributions made by patrons of the arts. The impressive heritage contained in the museum, occupying 140 exhibition rooms, has also been enriched further by the many archeological research activities undertaken in Brussels and abroad.

"Pursued Deers" (on the following pages), a piece donated by Lladró to the Bellevue Museum in 1987, now belongs to the permanent collection of the Fiftieth Anniversary Museum (above). Both institutions form part of the Royaux Musées of Art and History.

Among many other features, northern Italy boasts the picturesque region of Emilia, where the city of Faenza is located, famous for its tin-glazed earthenware.

Its majolica – or glazed pottery – tradition goes back to the 15th and

THE INTERNATIONAL CERAMICS MUSEUM OF FAENZA

16th centuries, explaining why this Mediterranean town houses one of the most important ceramics museums in the world. The founder of the museum was Gaetano Ballardini, a businessman who successfully brought about a renovation in artisan traditions at the beginning of this century, following a sharp decline in the late 19th century due to a serious structural crisis.

The history of the museum begins in 1908, the year in which Faenza, birthplace of the physicist and mathematician Evangelista Torricelli (1608-47), the inventor of the barometer, was named as the venue of an important agricultural and industrial fair held in honour of the third centenary of the famous physicist. Taking advantage of the moment and in collaboration with outstanding collectors, artists and companies in the trade, Ballardini ingeniously contrived to gather together an extensive collection of ceramics, comprising antiques and contemporary European pieces, which were exhibited at the fair. After the closure of the event, the indefatigable Ballardini installed the collection in a building donated by the city, where they have remained ever since, giving birth to the museum of Faenza.

Today, the International Ceramics Museum of Faenza is considered to be one of the most important museums of its kind on the international panorama. Among its permanent holdings, which have been increasing since its inception, are porcelain and ceramic objects from all ages plus examples from contemporary masters such as Picasso, Léger, Dalí, Chagall,

The Lladró sculpture entitled "Wrestling" (below) forms part of the permanent holdings of the museum of Faenza (on the following page), one of the most famous museums in the world for contemporary ceramics and porcelain.

Miró, Matisse and Melandri. Its ample international section includes pieces from around the world, and among other collections, the most famous are those dedicated to Far Eastern and Middle Eastern works.

Within the museum's magnificent halls there are authentic jewels of Pre-Columbian ceramic art, such as an anthropomorphic huaco from the Mochica civilization, found in Peru; majolica vases from the 14th and 15th centuries; a small 17th-century tray in the compendious style; and a Raphaelesque amphora decorated by Patanazzi in 1580.

Since it was founded, the museum has not only taken pains to gath-

er together the beautiful productions of the past in the form of ceramic art, but has also demonstrated its concerns to promote and foster artistic training. Thus, the museum's ceramics school was declared to be a Public Institute for Ceramic Arts in 1938. Today, the school's annual International Ceramics Competition is famous throughout the world.

Chosen by the current curator of the museum, Gian Carlo Bojani, who defined it as a work with "great expressive force and a magnificent execution", Lladró's sculpture called "Wrestling" has formed part of the museum's holdings since 1987.

This sculpture, belonging to a limited series of which there are only 50 in the entire world, now mostly in private collections, entered the select Lladró sculpture line in 1982.

"Wrestling" stand outs for its vigorous style and the forcefulness of its forms; it is a paradigm of expressiveness brought to life. With qualifications like these given by experts in sculpture, its place could be no other than the hall of a famous museum.

From June 16th to 30th 1994, the main hall of the Santo Domingo Modern Art Museum hosted the exhibition 'Lladró Close-Up' comprising twenty-five pieces, the majority of which came from the Elite series. The event received wide coverage in the Dominican media, causing a substantial amount of impact. As an anecdote, it is said that while a World Cup soccer match was being rebroadcast, the announcers took a pause to encourage TV viewers to visit the exhibition.

Lladró in World Museums

SANTO DOMINGO MODERN ART MUSEUM AND COLUMBUS' LIGHTHOUSE

Since 1994 the Lladró figurine "Pursued Deers" (below) has been on permanent exhibition at the Santo Domingo Modern Art Museum in the Dominican Republic. In the same year Lladró presented the Fifth Centenary Museum at Columbus' Lighthouse (following page) with "Spirit of America".

"Pursued Deers", one of the creations included in the exhibition, did not leave with the other pieces when the exhibition closed. Instead, it stayed behind to enter the museum's permanent holdings. During the closure of the event, the figurine was officially presented, in the presence of the Spanish Ambassador, to this Caribbean country.

In view of the exhibition's success, another piece entered the holdings of the Dominican monument dedicated to Columbus, a recently constructed lighthouse in the shape of a cross. This impressive building, erected to commemorate the Quincentenary of the Discovery of America and inaugurated by Pope John Paul II on October 11th 1992, contains representations from numerous Latin American countries in the form of permanent exhibitions. Since 1994, the "Spirit of America" figurine donated by Lladró occupies a privileged place in the main hall of the museum, located in the central transept of the building, which is dedicated to

Above, the Santo Domingo Modern Art Museum. On the following page, "Spirit of America", a work full of symbolism which seems to be almost tailor-made for the Dominican monument where it is on display.

Columbus and contains a number of valuable historic articles.

"Put crosses on all the roads and pathways so that God will bless them. This land belongs to Christians, and the memory of this must be preserved for all time." It was with words like these that Christopher Columbus announced his arrival to the New World. Five hundred years later, this idea is still apparent in the architectural form given to Columbus' Lighthouse.

Seen from the air, Columbus' Lighthouse is a huge cross laid out on the ground, an imperishable reproduction of the wooden crosses placed on all the islands and coastlines discovered by Columbus.

The building, in the style of the pyramids and other world landmarks, does not include much typical architecture. In general, it is a low, solid, compact structure. It is a sturdy stone construction capable of withstanding hurricanes and earthquakes, conceived to stand as a monument for eternity.

The building and its surroundings present an imposing picture. The entrances are enormous slots cut in the walls leading the visitor to the heart of the building. To the west, a road leads to a floodgate on the river Ozama, facing the city of Santo Domingo. A great paved cross, set in the middle of the International Park, which covers about 2,500 acres, is the centrepoint from which avenues branch out like spokes in a wheel, one for each republic on the New Continent.

This building is composed of a number of libraries and museums and houses a chapel. In the chapel pantheon lie the remains of the Discoverer of America with two soldiers on permanent guard duty. Just above the chapel

On this page and the next, views of the impressive architectural complex built in tribute to Columbus, where "Spirit of America" (above) is on exhibit.

and crowning the building is the Altar of Progress. By night, a revolving light projects an immense luminous cross over the sky of Santo Domingo.

Taken as a whole, the monument is a collection of symbolic images, and no less symbolic is the "Spirit of America" figurine, which represents the union of two cultures brought about by the events of 1492 with the arrival of Columbus to the New World.

The figurine was made to commemorate the Quincentenary of the Discovery of America and represents the cultural and commercial exchange that initiated this historic event. On the top of the piece, which rises up into the sky, there is a ship with three masts, one for each caravel that sailed off to uncharted lands. The sails are billowing in the wind, the winds of hope.

Five nymphs hold the composition up. They are not soldiers or sailors, and they do not form part of the group of adventurers. The creation provides a picture which is quite different from the idea of discovery as conquest. These five young ladies represent all those souls who came from the Old World looking for a new lease on life, people anxious for new opportunities in the newly discovered lands; men, women and children searching for a better and more prosperous future. Among them are various other symbols: the dove as an allegory of peace, the rudder symbolizing the new course followed by history after the Discovery and the anchor, representing the establishment of Old World culture on the New.

Fittingly, "Spirit of America" has taken up its abode in a place that seems to have been destined for it, a museum at Columbus' Lighthouse – a monument to the theme on which the figurine was based. Thanks to this creation, plus the figurine "Pursued Deers" – a museum piece twice over, as it also forms part of the holdings of the Fiftieth Anniversary Museum in Belgium – Lladró is now present in the major museum institutions of the Dominican Republic.

On September 18th, 1988, Doña Pilar de Borbón, sister to the King of Spain, cut the ribbon that inaugurated the Lladró Center in New York. This is the most important Lladró centre outside Spain within the proprietary network of stores and exhibition centres run by Lladró in dynamic, cosmopolitan locations throughout the world.

LLADRÓ CENTER IN NEW YORK

The Lladró Center, on 57th Street in New York City, between Fifth and Sixth Avenue, occupies a modern, eight-storey building. It was rehabilitated according to the original 1920 plans following a project by the architects Rafael Tamarit, a regular associate of Lladró, and author of the designs for the City of Porcelain, and Carlos Brillembourg, winner of the prestigious Architectural Record House Award and 40 under 40 Award, and member of the American Architects Institute.

Within its neoclassical façade, the past and present of Lladró can be seen on nine different floors, including an ample space dedicated to sales of current creations, as well as the headquarters of the Lladró Society on the East Coast of the U.S.A., an auditorium for cultural events and the very first Lladró museum in the world.

"Allegory to the Peace" is on exhibit at the Lladró Center in New York.

Without doubt the museum is one of the main attractions in the building. Three floors inside have been dedicated to an extensive retrospective figurine exhibition. In all there are over 1,000 pieces, among which are some of the first creations made by the founders in the 1940s. This enables visitors to see how Lladró works have evolved over practically five decades.

Contained in the museum are pieces that have marked turning points in their careers, paying testimony to innumerable moments of

inspiration. The fifth floor presents some authentic jewels from the past: tiles and plates painted by the Lladró brothers when they were students, vases fired in the rudimentary kiln they first built in the patio of their parents' home, hand-painted Valencian fans, and their very first porcelain pieces. All of these are works of great artistic and testimonial value, gathered together over the years with great effort, as many of them were one-off pieces which had to be recovered from private collections.

The passion for sculpture felt by the youngest of the three brothers, Vicente, can be seen in the display cases containing, among other pieces, two bronze busts of their parents Rosa Dolz and Juan Lladró. Nearby cases show the brothers' admiration for 18th-century European porcelain in the form of richly decorated vases, chubby cherubs, and ballerinas dressed in delicate porcelain tutus, representations of pastoral scenes, and many other pieces with decorations over the glaze, a technique employed during their initial years.

The museum holdings boast an extensive retrospective collection of Lladró figurines. Over 1,000 pieces, among which are some of the first pieces ever created by the founding brothers in the forties, give an overview of Lladró's development over five decades.

A tour of the two lower floors gives another overview of the stages through which Lladró works have passed: from classic, traditional and academic naturalism, to modern naturalism with reminiscences of a sentimental kind of neo-romanticism responding to popular appeal; from the urge to represent full, well-rounded figures, to the sharp elongations of the 1970s; from firing in various stages to high-temperature single-firing and the use of pastel tones.

Also on exhibit is the complete collection of Lladró Society figurines. Every new year since 1985, Society members have been able to include exclusive new figurines in their collections, made specially for them. Here, at this collectors' mecca, where Society members enjoy preferential treatment, they can see all the members-only pieces having been issued since the Society's inception.

Visiting the Lladró Center in New York is a way to take a trip through Lladró history. It is an essential rendezvous for porcelain art lovers, set in the heart of Manhattan.

The Lladró Center, on 57th Street, between Fifth and Sixth Avenues, occupies a modern building reconstructed according to an original design from the 1920s.

Translation by: Simon Stepney

© Photography: Enrique Carrazoni
  Excerpts:
  - Carlos Sanchís. Page 23 below.
  - Lladró archive. Pages 10, 11, 12,
  13, 14, 15, 16, 17, 18, 19, 22, 26,
  27, 28, 29, 30, 32, 33, 35, 36, 38,
  39, 40, 41, 42, 44, 46, 47, 48, 49,
  50, 51, 52, 53, 57, 58, 59, 60, 61,
  62, 63, 64, 65, 66, 67, 70, 75, 100,
  101, 104, 105, 106, 107, 112, 113,
  114, 115, 118, 119, 120, 121, 122,
  123, 124, 125, 259, 260, 261, 263,
  264, 265, 266, 267, 274, 275, 276,
  277, 278, 280, 281, 283, 284 and 285.